ASONS IN THE HOME

FA

SEASONS IN TH

FALL

CREATIVE
HOME
ARTS
—CLUB—

CREATIVE HOME ARTS LIE

CREATIVE
HOME
ARTS
—CLUB—

CREATIVE HOME ARTS CLUB
MINNETONKA, MINNESOTA

CREDITS

SEASONS IN THE HOME
FALL

Printed in 2004.

Tom Carpenter
Creative Director

Heather Koshiol
Managing Editor

Jennifer Weaverling
Senior Book Development Coordinator

Jenya Prosmitsky
Book Design

BatScanner Productions, Inc.
Book Production

1 2 3 4 5 6 7 8 / 08 07 06 05 04
ISBN 1-58159-226-4
© 2004 Creative Home Arts Club

Creative Home Arts Club
12301 Whitewater Drive
Minnetonka, Minnesota 55343
www.creativehomeartsclub.com

Contributing Writers

Jim Anderson	Nancy Maurer
Donna Balzer	Cheryl Natt
Rosalind Creasy	Cheryl Nelson
Jana Freiband	Yula Nelson
Zoe Graul	Barbara Pleasant
Robert Haehle	Marilyn Raff
Stephanie Hainsfurther	A. Cort Sinnes
Natalia Hamill	William Thomas
Becky Heath	Ruth Zavitz
Janet Loughrey	

Contributing Photographers

Phil Aarrestad
Bill Lindner Photography
Mark Macemon
Mowers Photography
Tad Ware

Additional Photography

Rob Cardillo	Brent Heath
David Cavagnaro	Saxon Holt
Walter Chandoha	Johnny's Selected Seeds
Crandall & Crandall	Bill Johnson
Rosalind Creasy	Dency Kane
Todd Davis	Janet Loughrey
Alan & Linda Detrick	Park Seed Company
Derek Fell	Barbara Pleasant
John Gregor	Amy Sumner
Harry Haralambou	

Special thanks to: Mike Billstein, Terry Casey, Janice Cauley and Sandy Zilka.

CONTENTS

Introduction 6

Chapter 1
Fall Cooking   8

Lox and Bagel Salad .10
Honey-Sesame Chicken Tenderloins 11
Figs with Cheese, Honey and Walnuts 13
Mexican Copanata .14
Roasted Poblano and Chile Mashed Potatoes 16
Corn Bread 18
Beets and Oranges .19
Savory Noodle Kugel 20
Thanksgiving Salad .21
Harvest "Thyme" Squash Soup 23
Herbed Tomato Gratin 24
Root Vegetable and Barley Soup 25
Caesar Salad 26
Curried Pilaf Salad .28
Red and White Endive Slaw with Walnuts and Apples 29
Fennel and Pear Salad 31
Turkey Club with Cranberry and BLT 33
Fajita Chicken in Pumpkin-Seed Sauce 34
Brown-Ale Shiitake Mushroom Chicken 35
Pork Chops with Dried-Apple Stuffing 36
Roast Chicken 38
Turkey with Spinach Tortellini and Fresh Oranges 40
Hot Pastrami Salad .41
Apple Date Pecan Cake with Caramel Sauce 42
Inside-Out Fig Bars .43
Pumpkin Swirl Cheesecake 45
Apple Cream Cheese Bars 46

Chapter 2
Fall Crafts   48

Java Fire Starter 50
Fall Leaf Stationery .53
Fall Balsam Wreath .56
Nature's Bounty Basket 59
Mini-Kindling Box 62
Halloween Trick-or-Treat Bag 65
Scarecrow Wall Hanging 68
Wire Luminaria 71

Fall Leaf Clay Pot 74
Red Twig Dogwood Bush 76

Chapter 3
Fall Decorating   78

Antique Potpourri Jar 80
Birdhouse Shoe Rack 83
Framed and Pressed Fall-Colored Leaves 88
Fall Guest Hand Towel 91
Dried Apple Garland 94
Pumpkin Container with Mum Plant 97
Witch Mobile 100
Fallen Leaves Table Topper 103
Etched Glass Candle Holder and Decorative Candle 106
Fall Chair Dressing 109

Chapter 4
Fall Gardening   112

Autumn Knot Garden 114
Late-Season Stunners 116
Autumn's Everlasting Annuals 120
Autumn Glory: Wildflower Gardens 122
Six Ways to Extend Your Veggie-Growing Season 126
An Easy Autumn To-Do List 128
Plant Now for Season-Long Bloom 130
Easy Color from Bulbs 136
Trees for Autumn Color 138
Annual Cutting Garden for Fall Bouquets 142

Chapter 5
Fall Entertaining   144

Kick-Off Party 146
Autumn Dinner Party 154
Take It Easy This Fall 162
A Very Scary Affair 170
Just Ducky Dinner .178

Index 186

FALL

INTRODUCTION

Fall is bittersweet: Just a little bitter because summer is fading and winter looms, but so very sweet because the world is vibrant with color and life.

Autumn truly is alive with beauty, and it simply makes a person feel good to see the bright leaves, smell the crisp breeze and feel a warm Indian summer sun on your face. It's the time of year when Creative Home Arts Club Members like you wake up in the morning and hit the ground running with a special energy that just gets things done.

That's why we made *Seasons in the Home — Fall*. Here are hundreds of ways you can put all your autumn energy to wonderful and creative use.

Cooking is a joy now. The kitchen is cool, a bounty of fruits and vegetables are at their fullest and finest, and warm, comforting food tastes exquisite.

Fall is a crafter's dream. With so many natural items at their peak of beauty, creating memorable craft projects is as good as it gets all year.

Autumn is for decorating too. With nights becoming longer, more time is spent indoors, and you want every room in your home to look great.

You can grow some of the year's most beautiful flowers in fall. And vegetables thrive in the cool air. You can even get ready for spring.

Fall brings grand entertaining opportunities too — from Halloween to classic Thanksgiving.

So don't let autumn sneak past you this year, or any year. Celebrate its glory with all the creative ideas and projects in *Seasons in the Home — Fall*.

F A L L
COOKING

Something about fall makes cooking now very special. Maybe it's because summer is over and a warm kitchen feels good on a bright and crisp day or a frosty and dark evening. Perhaps its because autumn's bounty of ingredients presents some of the year's finest opportunities for wholesome, comforting and delicious taste. Quite likely it's a little bit of both. And that's the basis behind the recipe ideas you'll find here.

Facing page: Pumpkin Swirl Cheesecake, page 44

LOX AND BAGEL SALAD

Served as a canapé with Champagne or on a bagel to enjoy with the Sunday paper on a crisp fall morning, smoked salmon always holds the center of attention. For a gathering, multiply the ingredients and serve on a large platter.

Cream Cheese Dressing

- ¾ cup (6 oz.) whipped cream cheese
- 2 tablespoons milk
- ¼ teaspoon salt
- ⅛ teaspoon freshly ground pepper
- 2 tablespoons snipped fresh chives

Salad

- 1 head Boston (bibb) lettuce, separated into leaves, washed and drained
- 4 oz. thinly sliced smoked salmon, shredded
- ½ red onion, cut in half, very thinly sliced
- 2 tomatoes, cut in half, very thinly sliced
- 1 cup (1½ oz.) packaged garlic-flavored bagel chips*

1 In blender, combine cream cheese, milk, salt and pepper. Cover; blend until smooth. Pour into small bowl; stir in chives. Cover; refrigerate until serving.

2 Line plates with lettuce. Drizzle each serving with 1 tablespoon of the dressing. (Dressing may be prepared, covered and refrigerated up to 1 day before serving.)

3 Arrange salmon, onion and tomatoes on top of lettuce; drizzle with remaining dressing. Sprinkle with bagel chips.

4 (¾-cup) servings.
Preparation time: 30 minutes.
Ready to serve: 30 minutes.
Per serving: 255 calories, 18 g total fat (10 g saturated fat), 55 mg cholesterol, 555 mg sodium, 2 g fiber.

Cooking Tip

* If bagel chips are unavailable, substitute 1 onion bagel, cut crosswise into very thin slices. Bake in single layer on baking sheet at 375°F for 5 minutes or until crisp.

Honey-Sesame Chicken Tenderloins

Add this to your fall party menu! The convenient chicken breast tenderloins frozen in bags at the supermarket are perfect to use in this recipe; if you prefer, cut chicken breast halves lengthwise into thirds.

Chicken
 1 lb. boneless skinless chicken breast tenderloins
 2 tablespoons sesame seeds
 1 tablespoon chopped fresh cilantro

Marinade
 1 teaspoon salt
 2 tablespoons low-sodium soy sauce
 2 tablespoons honey
 2 tablespoons dry sherry
 ½ teaspoon grated fresh ginger
 ½ teaspoon Aisan five-spice powder
 2 tablespoons vegetable oil

Plum Orange Sauce
 ½ cup orange marmalade
 1 cup plum sauce or plum preserves
 1 tablespoon cornstarch
 1 tablespoon sugar
 1 tablespoon rice wine vinegar or fresh lemon juice
 ⅛ teaspoon cayenne pepper

1 For Chicken: Rinse chicken and pat dry.

2 For Marinade: In 1½-quart casserole, combine salt, soy sauce, honey, sherry, ginger, five-spice powder and oil; mix well. Add chicken to marinade, turning to coat chicken evenly. Cover and refrigerate 2 hours, turning once or twice.

3 Meanwhile, prepare Plum Orange Sauce: In microwave-safe bowl, combine orange marmalade, plum sauce, cornstarch, sugar, vinegar and cayenne pepper. Microwave at High power 1 minute until sauce bubbles and thickens; cool. Let stand 15 to 20 minutes. Serve warm; extra dip can be covered and refrigerated up to 1 month.

4 Heat oven to 400°F. Remove chicken from marinade; discard marinade. Sprinkle chicken with sesame seeds. Bake, uncovered, about 15 minutes or until chicken is no longer pink in center. Cut each piece in half, crosswise; place in serving dish. Sprinkle with cilantro. Serve with Plum Orange Sauce.

24 appetizers.
Preparation time: 20 minutes.
Ready to serve: 2 hours, 25 minutes.
Per appetizer: 30 calories, 1 g total fat (1 g saturated fat), 10.5 mg cholesterol, 50 mg sodium, 0 g fiber.

FIGS WITH CHEESE, HONEY AND WALNUTS

Figs generally ripen about the time summer light takes on the golden hue that signals autumn's approach. Honey and walnuts complete the autumn cornucopia of tastes in this recipe.

8   fresh ripe figs, cut in half lengthwise
1   cup fromage blanc, fresh ricotta cheese or ¾ cup mascarpone
3   tablespoons honey, preferably dark honey, such as lavender
½   cup shelled walnuts, toasted*

Cooking Tip

* To toast walnuts, spread on baking sheet; bake at 375°F for 7 to 10 minutes or until lightly browned. Cool.

1 Arrange figs on platter or individual serving plates. Place cheese in center of platter or add a generous spoonful to individual plates. Drizzle honey over cheese and figs; add walnuts. Serve immediately.

4 servings.
Preparation time: 10 minutes.
Ready to serve: 20 minutes.
Per serving: 310 calories, 16 g total fat (6 g saturated fat), 30 mg cholesterol, 55 mg sodium, 4 g fiber.

MEXICAN COPANATA

Don't let this rather long list of ingredients scare you. All the chopping is done in the food processor, and if you like, 1 cup of frozen chopped onions may be substituted for 1 medium onion. Serve this zesty dip with warm pita bread triangles for an afternoon of fall football watching.

1	medium onion, cut into 1-inch pieces
4	plum tomatoes, cut into 1-inch pieces
4	tomatillos, cut into 1-inch pieces
¼	cup chopped fresh cilantro
3	tablespoons olive oil
1	eggplant, cut into 1-inch pieces
½	cup oil-cured ripe olives, pitted
½	cup tomato sauce
¼	cup tomato paste
3	tablespoons pine nuts
3	tablespoons dried currants
1	tablespoon cumin
½	teaspoon crushed red pepper
⅛	teaspoon salt (optional)

1 In food processor, coarsely chop onion, tomatoes and tomatillos. Add cilantro; process an additional 2 minutes. Set aside.

2 In large skillet, heat olive oil over medium-high heat until hot. Sauté eggplant 2 to 3 minutes or until just brown at edges.

3 Reduce heat to low; add chopped tomato mixture, olives, tomato sauce, tomato paste, pine nuts, currants, cumin and red pepper. Stir to mix well.

4 Cook slowly, stirring often, 20 to 30 minutes or until mixture has thickened. Sprinkle with salt, if desired. Serve at room temperature.

4 cups.
Preparation time: 25 minutes.
Ready to serve: 1 hour.
Per 1 cup: 70 calories, 4 g fat (0.5 g saturated fat), 0 mg cholesterol, 160 mg sodium, 2.5 g fiber.

Chef's Note

- Tomatillos are a popular ingredient in Mexican and Southwestern cuisine. They resemble little green tomatoes, but are covered with a papery husk that must be removed before use. Tomatillos add a unique fruity flavor to vegetable dips, salads and chilled soup.

ROASTED POBLANO AND CHILE MASHED POTATOES

Here's a heavenly and autumny recipe for mashed potatoes!

1	cup butter, divided
⅓	cup garlic cloves, peeled
1	poblano chile, stem and seeds removed
4 to 6	russet potatoes
1	tablespoon plus 1 teaspoon salt
¼	cup heavy cream
¼	teaspoon ground white pepper
1	tablespoon finely minced fresh cilantro

1 Heat oven to 325°F.

2 Place ½ cup of the butter, garlic and chile in small, covered ovenproof pot. Bake 1 hour.

3 Rinse potatoes under cold water; cut into quarters. Place potatoes in large pot. Add enough cold water to cover potatoes; add 1 tablespoon of the salt. Heat to a boil. Reduce heat and boil until potatoes are tender when poked with thin paring knife; drain. Let potatoes stand uncovered 3 to 5 minutes, allowing liquid to steam off.

4 Remove butter mixture from oven. In food processor, puree mixture to fine consistency. Add puree mixture to potatoes. Add remaining ½ cup of the butter, cream, remaining 1 teaspoon of the salt and pepper; mash until creamy. When finished mashing, fold in cilantro.

4 servings.
Preparation time: 15 minutes
Ready to serve: 1 hour, 15 minutes
Per serving: 150 calories, 13 g fat (8 g saturated fat), 35 mg cholesterol, 315 mg sodium, 1 g fiber.

CORN BREAD

Corn bread is as American as apple pie, and perfectly suited for autumn cooking. Southerners like their corn bread thin and crusty with just a hint of sweetness. Northerners like their corn bread thicker and sweeter, baked with equal quantities of flour and cornmeal. This particular corn bread is Yankee-style, but if desired, you can cut back the sugar to 2 tablespoons.

1   cup milk
2   eggs
¼   cup butter, melted
1   cup all-purpose flour
1   cup cornmeal
¼   cup sugar
1   tablespoon baking powder
½   teaspoon salt

1 Heat oven to 425°F. Spray 8-inch square pan with nonstick cooking spray.

2 In medium bowl, whisk together milk, eggs and butter. With fork, stir in flour, cornmeal, sugar, baking powder and salt just until moistened.

3 Pour into pan. Bake 20 to 25 minutes or until golden and toothpick inserted near center comes out clean.

4 Cut into squares. Serve hot with unsalted butter.

12 servings.
Preparation time: 10 minutes.
Ready to serve: 35 minutes.
Per serving: 155 calories, 5.5 g fat (3 g saturated fat), 50 mg cholesterol, 265 mg sodium, 1 g fiber.

Variations

- **Golden Kernel Corn Bread.** Add 1 cup fresh or thawed frozen corn to the dry ingredients.

- **Mexican Corn Bread.** Fold 1 (4-oz.) can drained, chopped green chiles and ½ cup (2 oz.) grated cheddar cheese into batter.

- **Corn Bread with Scallions and Peppers.** Add 1 thinly sliced scallion, ¼ cup chopped red bell pepper and ¾ teaspoon crushed fresh sage to the wet ingredients.

- **Tomato-Dill Corn Bread.** Add ⅓ cup chopped sun-dried tomatoes and 2 tablespoons chopped fresh dill to dry ingredients.

BEETS AND ORANGES

This colorful salad with contrasting flavor, color and texture is very Mediterranean in style. As the salad sits, the flavors become better and better. This recipe also makes a beautiful addition to a fall buffet table or potluck supper.

1	lb. red beets, stems trimmed to 1 inch above beets
¼	cup water
2	oranges
1	teaspoon ground cumin
½	teaspoon ground cardamom
½	teaspoon ground coriander
½	teaspoon salt
¼	teaspoon freshly ground pepper
1	tablespoon fresh lemon juice
2	tablespoons extra-virgin olive oil
½	cup (2 oz.) feta cheese, crumbled

1 Heat oven to 400°F. Place beets in 13x9-inch pan; add water. Cover with aluminum foil; bake 45 minutes to 1 hour or until tender. Let cool. Cut stem and root from beets; peel and slice.

2 Meanwhile, using sharp knife, peel oranges, cutting away all white pulp and thin outer membrane. Holding over bowl to catch juice, cut between inner membranes to loosen and remove segments. Reserve orange segments and ¼ cup juice.

3 In small skillet, toast cumin, cardamom and coriander over low heat until fragrant. Stir spices, salt, pepper and lemon juice into reserved ¼ cup orange juice. Pour mixture over beets; gently stir. Drizzle beets with olive oil; gently stir. (Beets can be prepared up to 24 hours ahead. Cover and refrigerate; bring to room temperature before serving.)

4 Arrange sliced beets and reserved orange segments on platter or 4 salad plates. Sprinkle with feta. Pour marinade from beets into small pitcher. Serve alongside salad.

4 servings.
Preparation time: 30 minutes.
Ready to serve: 1 hour, 45 minutes.
Per serving: 165 calories, 10 g total fat (3 g saturated fat), 10 mg cholesterol, 510 mg sodium, 3 g fiber.

SAVORY NOODLE KUGEL

This easy noodle pudding is pure comfort food. A sprinkling of grated lemon peel in the baking dish provides a subtle infusion of lemon that complements the fresh herbs of autumn.

2 teaspoons freshly grated lemon peel
  (yellow portion only)
2 slices whole wheat sandwich bread,
  crusts removed, torn into large pieces
2 teaspoons extra-virgin olive oil
1 (8-oz.) pkg. wide or medium egg noodles
2 large eggs
1½ cups reduced-fat (1 percent) cottage cheese
1 cup reduced-fat sour cream
¾ teaspoon salt
¼ teaspoon freshly ground pepper
½ cup trimmed chopped scallions
3 tablespoons chopped fresh parsley
3 tablespoons chopped fresh dill

1 Heat oven to 325°F. Spray 2-quart glass casserole with cooking spray. Sprinkle with lemon peel; set aside.

2 In food processor, grind bread into coarse crumbs. Add oil; pulse to blend.

3 Cook noodles according to package directions. Drain thoroughly under cold running water.

4 In large bowl, whisk eggs. Add cottage cheese, sour cream, salt and pepper; whisk until blended. Add scallions, parsley, dill and noodles; mix with rubber spatula. Scrape into casserole. Sprinkle evenly with reserved bread crumb mixture. (Kugel can be made ahead to this point. Cover and refrigerate up to 8 hours.)

5 Bake kugel 35 to 45 minutes or until lightly browned and set. Let cool 5 minutes before serving.

4 servings.
Preparation time: 20 minutes.
Ready to serve: 1 hour, 10 minutes.
Per serving: 435 calories, 12.5 g total fat (4.5 g saturated fat), 180 mg cholesterol, 1190 mg sodium, 3 g fiber.

Chef's Note

- You can substitute ricotta for cottage cheese, and ½ cup chopped fresh basil for the dill and parsley.

THANKSGIVING SALAD

The nutty taste of brown and wild rice announces autumn. So it's natural to combine these grains with turkey and cranberries. To save time, prepare and assemble the other ingredients while the rice cooks.

¾ cup brown rice
½ cup wild rice
2½ cups cold water
1 cup dried cranberries
1 cup (5 oz.) diced smoked turkey
1 tablespoon cider vinegar
1 tablespoon hot mustard
½ teaspoon salt
¼ teaspoon freshly ground pepper
¼ cup extra-virgin olive oil
9 cups arugula or mustard greens
2 tablespoons walnut oil or hazelnut oil

1 In medium saucepan, combine brown rice and wild rice. Add cold water. Bring to a boil; reduce heat to low. Simmer 45 minutes or until tender. Water should barely show bubbles as it simmers to prevent rice grains from breaking.

2 Drain rice; transfer to large bowl. Gently toss to cool. Stir in cranberries, turkey, vinegar, mustard, salt, pepper and olive oil. Let cool to room temperature or cover and refrigerate. (Salad can be prepared up to 12 hours ahead. Cover and refrigerate; bring to room temperature before serving.)

3 Place arugula in large bowl. Add walnut oil; toss to coat. Arrange about 1½ cups arugula on each of 6 salad plates. Top each with about ¾ cup rice mixture.

6 (¾-cup) servings.
Preparation time: 15 minutes.
Ready to serve: 1 hour.
Per serving: 360 calories, 15.5 g total fat (2 g saturated fat), 10 mg cholesterol, 530 mg sodium, 3.5 g fiber.

Harvest "Thyme" Squash Soup

Pears contribute an underlying sweetness to this luxurious squash soup. And what says "autumn!" better than squash? A thyme-infused cream swirl gives it a beautiful finish. Try infusing milk or cream with thyme when you are making mashed potatoes or cream sauce.

1	tablespoon olive oil
2	cups sliced leeks, white and light green parts only
2	lb. butternut squash, seeded, cut into 2-inch cubes*
2	firm ripe pears, such as Bartlett or Anjou, cored, diced
2	garlic cloves, crushed
1	tablespoon chopped fresh thyme or 1 teaspoon dried
2	(14.5-oz.) cans reduced-sodium chicken broth
1	cup water
¼	cup whipping cream
6	fresh thyme sprigs or 1 teaspoon dried
¼	cup low-fat plain yogurt or reduced-fat sour cream
1	tablespoon fresh lemon juice
¼	teaspoon salt
⅛	teaspoon freshly ground pepper
	Chopped fresh chives

1 In 4- to 6-quart soup pot, heat oil over medium heat. Add leeks; cook 3 to 4 minutes or until tender, stirring frequently. Add squash, pears, garlic and chopped thyme; cook 1 minute, stirring constantly. Add broth and water; bring to a simmer. Reduce heat to low. Simmer, covered, 30 minutes or until squash is tender.

2 Meanwhile, in small saucepan, heat cream until steaming. Remove from heat; add thyme sprigs. Cover and steep 20 minutes. Strain cream into small bowl, pressing on thyme to extract flavor. Add yogurt; whisk until smooth.

3 Strain soup through colander into large bowl. Place solids in food processor; process until smooth. Return puree and broth to soup pot; heat through. Stir in lemon juice; season with salt and pepper. (Soup can be prepared up to 2 days ahead. Cover and refrigerate.)

4 To serve, ladle soup into bowls; add large dollop (or several small dollops) of infused cream to each bowl. Draw tip of knife or toothpick through cream to make decorative swirls. Garnish with chives.

8 (1-cup) servings.
Preparation time: 30 minutes.
Ready to serve: 1 hour, 15 minutes.
Per serving: 145 calories, 5 g total fat (2 g saturated fat), 10 mg cholesterol, 525 mg sodium, 5 g fiber.

Cooking Tip

* To make a squash easier to peel, try this trick: Pierce squash in several places with a fork or skewer and microwave at High for 2 minutes just to soften skin. Let stand for several minutes. Use a vegetable peeler or paring knife to remove skin.

HERBED TOMATO GRATIN

This rustic gratin with a Provençal accent is a lovely accompaniment to grilled or roasted lamb or beef. Coating the gratin dish with a sprinkling of herbed bread crumbs is a flavorful way to absorb the tomato juices.

5   slices firm white sandwich bread, crusts trimmed, torn into pieces
1   tablespoon dried herbes de Provence
1   garlic clove, minced
2   tablespoons extra-virgin olive oil
4   medium tomatoes, cut into ½-inch slices
⅛   teaspoon salt
⅛   teaspoon freshly ground pepper

1 Heat oven to 425° F. Spray 2½-quart gratin dish or shallow casserole with nonstick cooking spray.

2 In food processor, process bread until it breaks down into coarse crumbs. Add herbes de Provence and garlic; process until blended. Add oil; pulse several times.

3 Sprinkle ½ cup of the bread crumb mixture evenly over bottom of gratin dish. Bake crumbs 6 to 8 minutes or until light golden.

4 Arrange tomato slices, slightly overlapping, over crumbs; season with salt and pepper. Sprinkle with remaining bread crumb mixture; return gratin to oven. Bake 20 to 30 minutes or until golden.

4 servings.
Preparation time: 15 minutes.
Ready to serve: 45 minutes.
Per serving: 155 calories, 8 g total fat (1 g saturated fat), 0.5 mg cholesterol, 215 mg sodium, 2 g fiber.

ROOT VEGETABLE AND BARLEY SOUP

Nutty barley and root vegetables make a homey soup with an old-fashioned flavor. A splash of lemon juice and a generous sprinkling of dill give it a lively finish.

2	teaspoons olive oil
1	large onion, chopped
3	garlic cloves, minced
½	cup pearl barley
6	cups reduced-sodium chicken broth
2	medium carrots, diced
2	medium parsnips, diced
2	cups diced cooked chicken or turkey
⅓	cup chopped fresh dill
2	teaspoons fresh lemon juice
¼	teaspoon freshly ground pepper

1 In 4- to 6-quart soup pot, heat oil over medium heat until hot. Add onion; cook 2 to 3 minutes or until tender, stirring constantly. Add garlic; cook 30 seconds, stirring constantly. Add barley; stir to coat. Add broth; bring to a simmer. Reduce heat to low; skim off any foam. Simmer, covered, 20 minutes.

2 Add carrots and parsnips; simmer, covered, 15 to 20 minutes or until barley and vegetables are just tender. Add chicken; simmer an additional 3 to 4 minutes or until heated through. Stir in dill, lemon juice and pepper.

8 (1-cup) servings.
Preparation time: 20 minutes.
Ready to serve: 1 hour.
Per serving: 185 calories, 4.5 g total fat (1 g saturated fat), 30 mg cholesterol, 400 mg sodium, 4 g fiber.

Chef's Note

- To shorten cooking time, substitute quick-cooking barley for pearl barley; add carrots and parsnips with barley and simmer soup for a total of 20 minutes.

Caesar Salad

The original Caesar salad did not contain any anchovies. It was simply romaine lettuce tossed with top-quality ingredients: extra-virgin olive oil, salt, fresh ground pepper, fresh lemon juice, a few drops of Worcestershire sauce, raw eggs and Parmesan cheese ... then topped with croutons.

Salad

1	head romaine lettuce, torn into 1-inch pieces
6	anchovies, chopped
2	cups croutons
¼	cup (1 oz.) freshly grated Parmesan cheese

Dressing

2	egg whites
4	tablespoons fresh lemon juice
¼	teaspoon dry mustard
¼	teapoon sugar
¼	teaspoon hot pepper sauce
½	teaspoon garlic powder
½	cup peanut oil

1 For Salad: Place greens in large bowl; add anchovies, croutons and Parmesan cheese.

2 For Dressing: In small saucepan, whisk together egg whites, lemon juice, mustard, sugar, hot pepper sauce and garlic powder over low heat. Stir constantly until mixture thickens. Remove from heat.

3 Set saucepan over ice water 1 minute to stop cooking. Let stand at room temperature 5 minutes. Transfer to large bowl; slowly whisk in oil. Pour dressing over salad.

4 servings.
Preparation time: 15 minutes.
Ready to serve: 35 minutes.
Per serving: 430 calories, 37.5 g total fat (8 g saturated fat), 130 mg cholesterol, 475 mg sodium, 3 g fiber.

CURRIED PILAF SALAD

While this dish resembles a hot rice pilaf, it makes a delicious salad when served chilled or at room temperature. For the best flavor, choose a good quality curry powder. To avoid overcooking the rice, test a few grains after about 15 minutes of cooking. For salads, the rice should be just a bit chewy.

1 tablespoon vegetable oil
½ cup finely chopped onion
2 garlic cloves, minced
1 tablespoon curry powder
1 cup basmati or long-grain white rice, rinsed,
    drained
1 (15½-oz.) can chicken broth (about 2 cups)
½ teaspoon salt
1 cup pitted dates, chopped
¼ cup finely chopped fresh curly parsley
¼ cup toasted pine nuts or slivered almonds

1 In heavy 3-quart saucepan, heat oil over medium-high heat until hot. Add onion; cook, stirring constantly, 3 minutes. Add garlic and curry powder; cook, stirring constantly, 1 minute or until onion is tender and curry is fragrant.

2 Stir in rice. Cook, stirring constantly, 1 minute. Stir in broth and salt; bring to a simmer. Reduce heat to medium-low. Simmer, covered, 20 to 30 minutes or just until rice is tender and liquid is absorbed.

3 Transfer rice mixture to large bowl. Using large wooden spoon, gently stir and toss to cool. Stir in dates, parsley and pine nuts. Let cool to room temperature. (Salad can be prepared up to 24 hours ahead. Cover and refrigerate; bring to room temperature before serving.)

6 (1-cup) servings.
Preparation time: 20 minutes.
Ready to serve: 50 minutes.
Per serving: 275 calories, 6.5 g total fat (1 g saturated fat), 0 mg cholesterol, 515 mg sodium, 4 g fiber.

Chef's Note

• For an entrée salad, stir in 1 cup diced, cooked turkey or chicken. Serve on bed of greens.

RED AND WHITE ENDIVE SLAW WITH WALNUTS AND APPLES

It's not just Belgian anymore! Thanks to a California innovator, beautiful endive is now produced in our own country. This is a great salad for entertaining because it can be tossed and refrigerated for 2 or 3 hours, then arranged just before serving.

Lemon and Honey Dressing
2 teaspoons freshly grated lemon peel
3 tablespoons fresh lemon juice
2 teaspoons honey
¼ teaspoon salt
⅛ teaspoon ground white pepper
2 tablespoons extra-virgin olive oil

Salad
2 red endives or 1 head radicchio
2 white endives
½ bulb fennel, white part only, cut into matchstick-size strips (¼x¼x1-inch)
1 crisp apple, such as Gala or Granny Smith, cut into matchstick-size strips (¼x¼x1-inch)
½ cup toasted walnuts
½ cup (2 oz.) crumbled Gorgonzola cheese

1 In small bowl, combine lemon peel, lemon juice, honey, salt and pepper. Whisk in olive oil.

2 Reserve 8 whole red endive leaves and 8 white leaves. Gently rinse, dry and wrap in paper towel; refrigerate until serving. Gently rinse and dry remaining endive leaves; cut crosswise into thin slivers.

3 In large bowl, combine slivered endive leaves, fennel, apple and walnuts. Toss with dressing. Arrange 2 red and 2 white endive leaves on each of 4 salad plates. Place about ½ cup slivered endive mixture in center of each plate. Sprinkle each serving with Gorgonzola.

4 servings.
Preparation time: 20 minutes.
Ready to serve: 20 minutes.
Per serving: 250 calories, 19.5 g total fat (5 g saturated fat), 12.5 mg cholesterol, 405 mg sodium, 4 g fiber.

FENNEL AND PEAR SALAD

This fresh-tasting salad is perfect for fall. To prevent fennel and pear slices from browning, immediately toss them with rice vinegar. You may refrigerate the salad for an hour or two, but add the blue cheese just before serving.

½ bulb fennel, trimmed just below green stems and above root end, cut into quarters
2 crisp red pears, halved, cored
3 tablespoons seasoned rice vinegar
1 tablespoon hazelnut oil or walnut oil
⅛ teaspoon salt
⅛ teaspoon freshly ground pepper
1 head butter lettuce, separated into leaves
¼ cup (2 oz.) crumbled blue cheese

1 Using mandoline or very sharp knife, cut fennel into paper-thin slices. Place in large bowl.

2 Quarter pears; cut into very thin, lengthwise slices. Add pears and vinegar to fennel; gently toss. Add oil, salt and pepper; toss again.

3 Arrange lettuce on 4 salad plates. Top with fennel and pear slices. Sprinkle with blue cheese.

4 (½-cup) servings.
Preparation time: 15 minutes.
Ready to serve: 15 minutes.
Per serving: 125 calories, 6.5 g total fat (2 g saturated fat), 5 mg cholesterol, 205 mg sodium, 3.5 g fiber.

Chef's Note

- To create lovely pear slices, cut a pear into halves, lengthwise. Remove the core using melon ball scoop or grapefruit spoon. Gently pull away the stem.

TURKEY CLUB WITH CRANBERRY AND BLT

This is a favorite day-after-Thanksgiving sandwich in many households. Some people like

to add a layer of turkey dressing in place of the center bread slice in this triple-decker.

12	slices whole wheat bread, toasted
6	tablespoons butter, softened
¾	cup whole cranberry sauce
8	lettuce leaves
½	lb. cooked turkey, thinly sliced
4	thin slices sweet red onion
8	slices cooked bacon

1 Spread each slice of toast with ½ tablespoon butter and 1 tablespoon cranberry sauce.

2 Layer toast, lettuce, turkey, toast, lettuce, onion, 2 slices bacon and toast for each sandwich.

3 Cut sandwich into quarters to serve.

4 sandwiches.
Preparation time: 5 minutes.
Ready to serve: 5 minutes.
Per sandwich: 625 calories, 31 g total fat (15 g saturated fat), 104.5 mg cholesterol, 825 mg sodium, 7.5 g fiber.

Fajita Chicken in Pumpkin-Seed Sauce

When pumpkin seeds (maybe those left from your Halloween jack-o-lantern) are pureed with green chiles and cilantro, they turn into a delicate green sauce. These fajitas are great for a casual party menu. Have guests spoon the chicken into warm flour tortillas and add toppings.

½ cup roasted, salted pumpkin seeds*
¼ cup blanched, slivered, almonds
¼ teaspoon cumin seeds
½ small onion, cut up
1 garlic clove
1 (4-oz.) can chopped green chiles
½ cup packed fresh cilantro leaves
2 cups chicken broth
2 tablespoons olive oil
4 large skinless boneless chicken breast halves, rinsed and cut crosswise into ½-inch strips
1 tablespoon lemon juice
Warm flour tortillas
Shredded lettuce
Chopped tomato
Sour cream
Sliced avocado
Sliced jalapeño peppers

1 In heavy skillet, cook pumpkin seeds, almonds and cumin seeds over medium heat until toasted.

2 Transfer mixture to food processor. Add onion, garlic, chiles, cilantro and 1 cup of the broth, process until smooth. Set aside.

3 Add oil to skillet and heat for 1 minute; add chicken, the remaining 1 cup of the broth, juice and pumpkin sauce. Simmer, uncovered, 15 minutes or until chicken is no longer pink in center.

4 Spoon chicken mixture into tortillas; garnish with lettuce, tomato, sour cream, avocado and jalapeño peppers.

4 servings.
Preparation time: 15 minutes.
Ready to serve: 30 minutes.
Per serving: 575 calories, 30 g total fat (6.5 g saturated fat), 85 mg cholesterol, 1120 mg sodium, 500 g fiber.

Cooking Tip

* Pumpkin seeds are available in whole foods markets as well as in bulk-bin sections of many large supermarkets.

BROWN-ALE SHIITAKE MUSHROOM CHICKEN

Brown ale gives the sauce a lovely, creamy tan color and an elusive but exciting bite reflective of the bite in the crisp fall air. Serve this quick-to-prepare dish with rice pilaf and stir-fried autumn vegetables such as zucchini and the year's final peppers.

2	tablespoons butter
2	tablespoons all-purpose flour
½	teaspoon salt
½	teaspoon pepper
4	boneless skinless chicken breast halves
3½	oz. fresh shiitake mushrooms, sliced, stems removed
2	tablespoons finely chopped onion
½	cup brown ale
1	tablespoon Dijon mustard
½	cup whipping cream

1 In heavy skillet, heat butter over medium-high heat until melted. In small bowl, combine flour, salt and pepper; mix well. Dip chicken into mixture and place in skillet. Add mushrooms and onion. Cook chicken about 20 minutes or until chicken is no longer pink in center.

2 Add ale to skillet; cook an additional 5 minutes. Add mustard and whipping cream; simmer until sauce is pale tan and is consistency of heavy cream.

3 Transfer chicken to serving platter; spoon sauce and mushrooms over chicken.

4 servings.
Preparation time: 10 minutes.
Ready to serve: 25 minutes.
Per serving: 304 calories, 18.5 g total fat (10.5 g saturated fat), 115 mg cholesterol, 305 mg sodium, 1 g fiber.

Pork Chops with Dried-Apple Stuffing

For this old-fashioned autumn dish, choose chops ¾ to 1 inch thick, so that a pocket can

be cut in each. Usually the butcher will oblige, or you can do it yourself (see tip).

½   cup dried apples, cut into ½-inch pieces
½   cup apple cider or apple juice
3   tablespoons vegetable oil
3   large shallots, chopped
¼   cup chopped celery
1   cup fresh brown bread crumbs
¾   teaspoon dried sage
4   (8-oz.) center-cut pork chops
⅛   teaspoon salt
⅛   teaspoon freshly ground pepper
¼   cup water

1 Place apples in small bowl; pour cider over apples. Microwave at High power 1½ minutes; drain and set aside, reserving liquid.

2 In medium skillet, heat 2 tablespoons of the oil over medium-high heat until hot. Sauté shallots and celery until shallots begin to brown. Remove from heat. Add bread crumbs, sage, well-drained dried apples and just enough apple liquid to moisten; mix well.

3 Heat broiler. Cut pocket in each pork chop.* Stuff mixture into pockets. Brush with remaining 1 tablespoon of the oil; sprinkle with salt and pepper. Arrange in 13x9-inch pan; place under broiler 1 to 2 minutes or until brown.

4 Heat oven to 350°F. Secure stuffed pockets with toothpicks. Pour water into pan; cover tightly with aluminum foil. Bake 30 minutes. Uncover and bake an additional 20 minutes or until internal temperature reaches at least 160°F.

4 servings.
Preparation time: 15 minutes.
Ready to serve: 1 hour, 15 minutes.
Per serving: 550 calories, 30 g fat (8.5 g saturated fat), 100 mg cholesterol, 380 mg sodium, 2.5 g fiber.

Cooking Tip

* Make a pocket by using a sharp knife to cut towards the bone.

ROAST CHICKEN

The perfect meal for company ... or for yourself after a day raking leaves. Roasting breast side down during the first 30 minutes of cooking time will help keep the meat juicy and flavorful, but basting is essential for a moist, tender chicken. Baste often (about every 15 minutes) using oil, butter, stock or pan drippings. Plan on approximately ½ cup stuffing per pound of poultry.

1	(3½-lb.) fryer-broiler chicken
⅛	teaspoon salt
⅛	teaspoon freshly ground pepper
2	garlic cloves, halved
½	lemon, cut into 2 or 3 pieces
1	sprig rosemary or thyme
2	tablespoons vegetable oil

1 Heat oven to 375°F.

2 Remove excess fat and giblets; set giblets aside. Wash chicken and pat dry. Season inside cavity with salt and pepper. Tuck in garlic, lemon and rosemary. Secure drumsticks with string.

3 Place chicken, breast side down, on rack set in baking pan; brush with oil. Bake 30 minutes, basting once or twice with pan juices.

4 Turn chicken breast side up. Reduce heat to 350°F. Continue baking, basting often, an additional 45 minutes to 1 hour or until internal temperature reaches 180°F. Let stand at room temperature 10 to 15 minutes before carving.

4 servings.
Preparation time: 15 minutes.
Ready to serve: 2 hours.
Per serving: 445 calories, 27 g fat (7 g saturated fat), 145 mg cholesterol, 710 mg sodium, 0 g fiber.

Variations

- **Simple Crouton Stuffing.** Omit garlic and lemon from Roast Chicken. To make the stuffing, sauté 1 chopped small onion and 1 rib chopped celery in ¼ cup margarine. Remove from heat; fold in 2 cups seasoned croutons, ¼ teaspoon ground thyme and about 3 tablespoons reduced-sodium chicken broth (enough to moisten stuffing). If you don't have chicken broth, mix 3 tablespoons water with 1 teaspoon Worcestershire sauce. Stuff loosely into cavity. Secure drumsticks with string. Bake as directed for Roast Chicken until internal temperature reaches at least 180°F.

TURKEY WITH SPINACH TORTELLINI AND FRESH ORANGES

This is a great way to serve leftover cooked turkey … or you might want to make it especially for this recipe! Either way, buy fresh cheese-filled spinach tortellini in the market's dairy section.

3   large seedless oranges
7   cups homemade turkey or chicken broth
1½ pounds fresh cheese-filled spinach tortellini
3   cups cooked, diced or shredded turkey
2   cups sour cream
2   green onions, thinly sliced
    Freshly shredded Parmesan cheese

1 With vegetable peeler, remove 6x1-inch strip of peel from all 3 oranges. Cut strips into long, thin shreds and set aside. Peel oranges; cut crosswise into ¼-inch slices. Arrange slices on edges of serving platter.

2 In 8-quart stockpot, bring broth to a rolling boil. Add tortellini; cook according to package directions. Remove tortellini; set aside and keep warm.

3 Add turkey and orange peel shreds to broth; cook just until turkey is heated through. Remove turkey; add to tortellini.

4 In small skillet, combine sour cream with ½ cup broth and green onions; mix well. Heat mixture until just warm.

5 Spoon tortellini and turkey onto orange-lined serving platter; spoon sauce over tortellini. Serve with Parmesan cheese.

6 servings.
Preparation time: 10 minutes.
Ready to serve: 20 minutes.
Per serving: 485 calories, 25.5 g total fat (14 g saturated fat), 202 mg cholesterol, 135 mg sodium, 3 g fiber.

HOT PASTRAMI SALAD

You can think of this as either a salad or as a make-it-yourself sandwich. Either way, it's reminiscent of a New York deli and perfect for an autumn meal.

Honey Mustard Dressing
⅓   cup cider vinegar
¼   cup sweet hot mustard
¼   cup honey
2   teaspoons prepared horseradish (optional)
½   teaspoon salt

Salad
6   cups chopped iceberg lettuce
8   oz. thinly sliced pastrami, cut into strips, warmed if desired
1   cup miniature pretzels
8   dill pickle spears
4   slices toasted rye bread, each cut in half

1 In small bowl or pitcher, combine vinegar, mustard, honey, horseradish and salt.

2 In large bowl, combine lettuce and ¼ cup of the dressing; toss well. Divide lettuce among 4 salad plates.

3 Arrange pastrami over lettuce. Drizzle each serving with 1 tablespoon of the dressing. Sprinkle with pretzels. Garnish each plate with 2 pickle spears and 2 halves rye toast.

4 servings.
Preparation time: 15 minutes.
Ready to serve: 15 minutes.
Per serving: 380 calories, 18.5 g total fat (6 g saturated fat), 50 mg cholesterol, 2140 mg sodium, 4 g fiber.

APPLE DATE PECAN CAKE WITH CARAMEL SAUCE

A delicious way to use fall's best apples. A bit of cocoa and coffee in the batter heightens the flavor of the fruit. This moist yet crunchy cake is delicious served with warm Caramel Sauce.

Cake

1	cup sugar
½	cup (1 stick) butter, at room temperature
2	eggs
1½	cups all-purpose flour
2	teaspoons unsweetened cocoa
1	teaspoon baking soda
1	teaspoon ground cinnamon
½	teaspoon ground cloves
2	cups peeled, chopped, tart cooking apples
½	cup chopped pitted dates
1	cup coarsely chopped pecans
½	cup cold coffee

Caramel Sauce

¼	cup (½ stick) butter
½	cup packed brown sugar
½	cup whipping cream
1	teaspoon vanilla

1 Heat oven to 350°F. Lightly grease 10-inch springform pan or 13x9-inch pan.

2 In mixing bowl, beat sugar and ½ cup butter at medium speed until light and fluffy; beat in eggs until light. In separate bowl, combine flour, cocoa, baking soda, cinnamon and cloves.

3 In small bowl, combine apples, dates and pecans. Mix 2 tablespoons of the flour mixture into apples until all pieces are coated with flour. Mix remaining flour into butter mixture alternately with coffee until batter is smooth. Stir in apple mixture until well blended. Pour batter into pan; bake 35 to 40 minutes or until cake bounces back when touched in center. Cut cake into wedges while still warm; serve with warm Caramel Sauce.

4 To make Caramel Sauce: In small saucepan, melt ¼ cup butter. Stir in brown sugar over low heat 2 minutes until sugar is dissolved. Add cream; heat just to a boil. Remove from heat; stir in vanilla. Serve warm.

12 servings.
Preparation time: 40 minutes.
Ready to serve: 2 hours, 10 minutes.
Per serving: 580 calories, 23 g total fat (10 g saturated fat), 80 mg cholesterol, 200 mg sodium, 7.5 g fiber.

INSIDE-OUT FIG BARS

Remember that old favorite, the Fig Newton? A version of this retro favorite, these cookies offer an ooey-gooey fig center "filling" that tops a crunchy, cake-like crust. To finish it off, these bars — which are filled with the flavors of the harvest — are sprinkled lightly with powdered sugar.

Filling
  1   cup dried figs
  ¼   cup almonds
  ¼   cup raisons
  ¼   cup apricot preserves
  ½   teaspoon ground cinnamon

Dough
  2   cups all-purpose flour
  ¼   cup sugar
  ¾   teaspoon baking powder
  ½   teaspoon salt
  ½   cup (1 stick) butter
  2   eggs

Topping
  ¼   cup powdered sugar

1 Heat oven to 350°F. Line baking sheets with parchment paper.

2 In food processor, pulse figs, almonds and raisins until mixture crumbles. Add apricot preserves and cinnamon; pulse until combined. Set aside.

3 In large mixing bowl, combine flour, sugar, baking powder and salt. Using pastry blender or fork, cut butter into dry ingredients. Beat in eggs at medium speed until dough forms a ball on paddle.

4 Roll ¼ of dough at a time on lightly floured surface to ¼ inch thick. Cut 12 (2-inch) circles from dough. Top each circle with rounded ½ teaspoonful filling. Re-roll dough to cut more circles if necessary. Repeat with remaining dough and filling. Place cookies on baking sheets.

5 Bake one sheet at a time 12 to 15 minutes or until bottoms of cookies are golden brown. Cool slightly; sprinkle with powdered sugar. Transfer to wire rack to cool completely.

4 dozen cookies.
Preparation time: 30 minutes.
Ready to serve: 2 hours.
Per cookie: 70 calories, 2.5 g total fat (1 g saturated fat), 15 mg cholesterol, 405 mg sodium, 1 g fiber.

PUMPKIN SWIRL CHEESECAKE

There is a cheesecake for every season. This recipe will certainly be dessert-of-the-day for autumn celebrations.

Crust
1½ cups graham cracker crumbs
3 tablespoons sugar
6 tablespoons butter or margarine, melted

Filling
3 (8-oz.) pkg. cream cheese, softened
¾ cup sugar
3 tablespoons all-purpose flour
3 eggs
½ cup sour cream
1½ teaspoons vanilla
¼ cup packed brown sugar
¾ teaspoon ground cinnamon
½ teaspoon ground nutmeg
½ teaspoon ginger
½ teaspoon allspice
1½ cups pumpkin puree
2 tablespoons maple syrup

Topping
1 cup sour cream
2 tablespoons packed brown sugar

Garnish
⅓ cup pecan halves, sugared if desired

1 Heat oven to 325°F. In medium bowl, combine graham cracker crumbs, 3 tablespoons sugar and butter; mix until blended. Press crumb mixture into bottom and up sides of 9-inch springform pan. Bake 10 minutes. Remove from oven; cool.

2 In mixing bowl, combine cream cheese, ¾ cup sugar and 2 tablespoons of the flour; beat at medium speed until well blended. Add eggs, one at a time, mixing well after each addition. Blend in ½ cup sour cream and vanilla. Remove approximately 3 cups batter; set aside.

3 In medium bowl, combine ¼ cup brown sugar, the remaining 1 tablespoon of the flour, cinnamon, nutmeg, ginger and allspice; mix to blend. Mix pumpkin, brown sugar mixture and maple syrup into remaining batter; stir until blended. Spoon ½ of pumpkin mixture into crust. Gently spoon ½ of plain batter over pumpkin batter. Continue alternating layers of batter until pan is full. With metal spatula or knife, gently swirl spatula through batters for marbled effect. Bake 1 hour 5 minutes or until center is set. Remove from oven; loosen cake from rim of pan. Cool completely before removing rim of pan. Chill several hours or overnight.

4 In small bowl, combine 1 cup sour cream and 2 tablespoons brown sugar. Spread on top of cooled cheesecake. Top with pecans. Store in refrigerator.

12 servings.
Preparation time: 40 minutes.
Ready to serve: 3 hours, 25 minutes.
Per serving: 500 calories, 35.5 g total fat (20.5 g saturated fat), 150 mg cholesterol, 300 mg sodium, 1.5 g fiber.

APPLE CREAM CHEESE BARS

Enjoy these cheesecake-y bars with an apple-y fall twist on-the-go, in brown bag lunches or as a late day snack. Although not as formal as traditional cheesecake, they're definitely as tasty!

Crust

1½	cups all-purpose flour
½	cup packed light brown sugar
¼	cup (½ stick) butter or margarine
1	egg
1	teaspoon vanilla

Filling

1	(8-oz.) pkg. cream cheese
¼	cup plus ⅓ cup sugar
1	egg
½	teaspoon vanilla
2½	cups thinly sliced peeled baking apples
1	tablespoon lemon juice
1	teaspoon ground cinnamon
1	teaspoon ground nutmeg
	Caramel or butterscotch ice cream topping (optional)

1 Heat oven to 400°F. In mixing bowl, combine flour, brown sugar, butter, egg and 1 teaspoon vanilla; beat at medium speed until crumbly. Press crumb mixture into bottom and up sides of 8- or 9-inch square pan. Bake 6 to 8 minutes or until lightly browned. Remove from oven; cool.

2 Increase oven temperature to 450°F. In another medium bowl, combine cream cheese and ¼ cup of the sugar; mix well. Mix in egg and ½ teaspoon vanilla until well blended.

3 In separate bowl, toss apples with lemon juice. Add the remaining ⅓ cup of the sugar, cinnamon and nutmeg; mix lightly. Pour cream cheese mixture into crust; spoon apple mixture over cream cheese. Bake 10 minutes. Reduce oven temperature to 400°F; bake an additional 25 minutes or until knife inserted in center comes out clean. Cool. Cut into squares. Serve with warm ice cream topping, if desired. Store in refrigerator.

9 servings.
Preparation time: 35 minutes.
Ready to serve: 2 hours, 15 minutes.
Per serving: 345 calories, 15.5 g total fat (9 g saturated fat), 90 mg cholesterol, 130 mg sodium, 1.5 g fiber.

FALL CRAFTS

F all offers up some of the year's most fun and pretty items of natural beauty, just ready to incorporate into exciting craft projects. There are colorful leaves, of course. But also pine cones. Flowers. Fruits. Nuts. And an entire cornucopia of additional "ingredients" just begging to be put to good use on craft creations of exquisite beauty. Here are the exciting autumn craft ideas you need.

Facing page: Nature's Bounty Basket, page 59

JAVA FIRE STARTER

Create a fire starter for wood-burning fireplaces using recycled products from your home! Old coffee grounds, candle wax and recycled paper combine to form a mold. Place several starter molds in a small basket to give as a gift.

The Java Fire Starter gives off a slight coffee scent when burning. Or you can add other favorite scents to the wax instead. It's a great way to make use of material that would otherwise be thrown away. By limiting the amount of wax used, you can ensure that the mold will burn cleanly in most fireplaces.

This project will take approximately 2 hours to complete.

Select materials that have already been used to avoid further expense. Candle wax can be purchased in most craft stores or online on the Internet for about $2.00 per pound, but old candles work just as well. If you want to use colored shredded paper instead of recycled paper, you can purchase it at most craft stores for about $2.00. Use recycled margarine bowls for the molds and empty coffee cans for mixing the materials.

1 Wash and dry an empty coffee can. Break wax into chunks using a hammer and chisel. Fill the empty coffee can with chunks of wax. Put the can in a larger pan filled with water.

2 Place the pan on an electric burner until water begins to boil, then reduce the heat to an easy boil until the wax in the coffee can melts. Put a handful of shredded paper and a cup of dried, used coffee in a second coffee can. Pour the liquid wax over the paper and coffee grounds and stir quickly.

3 Before the wax cools or hardens, pour the wax mixture into empty margarine bowls. Using a large spoon, press the mixture down into the cup to mold tightly. Pour a very small amount of melted wax over the mixture to set the mold. Place mixture into the freezer for 10 to 20 minutes. Remove the contents from each mold and place in a fabric-lined basket to display by the fireplace.

Craft Tips

- To use, place the starter under the wood in a fireplace (or open pit outdoors) and light with a match. The mold will burn for up to 30 minutes by itself, but when placed under the wood it will start the wood burning in only a few minutes.

- Other flammable ingredients can also be added to the recipe, as you prefer. Be creative. Try dried leaves to add color to your molds. Test molds outdoors to make sure they burn cleanly before using in your fireplace.

- Use the wax in small quantities to avoid buildup on the bottom of your fireplace. The wax evaporates or burns off after the wood logs have started to burn. The small amount of ash created by the paper and coffee can be removed with the wood ash.

- Coffee burns better and releases more energy than wood. If you have large amounts of coffee available, experiment with larger molds that can be burned by themselves.

FALL LEAF STATIONERY

It is pure pleasure to create something beautiful as well as functional. Making cards using rubber stamps while mixing in a little homemade craftiness and creativity results in just that. This is an easily satisfying project that will make a great card to give to that special someone.

Sending a homemade card to someone really lets them know you care — it is truly like sending a little piece of yourself. There are endless ways to create cards using rubber stamps. Once you get started with this idea, you will be well on your way to envisioning your own creations. Using a simple leaf stamp, some card stock, embossing powder and inexpensive tools found at most craft stores, you'll make these cards in no time at all.

This project will take approximately 1 to 2 hours to complete and cost about $15.00.

Materials & Tools

- Fall leaf-shaped rubber stamp, in assorted sizes if desired
- Multicolored ink pad or pads in dark fall colors, such as deep blue and red
- 5½-inch square blank note cards with envelopes
- Embossing ink pad
- 8½- by 10-inch sheets card stock for gold leaf cutouts
- Gold embossing powder
- Two-way glue stick
- 4½-inch squares card stock (two per card)
- 3½-inch squares card stock (two per card)
- Script stamp (such as "Thank You"), if desired for inside of card
- Heavy-duty mounting squares and/or multi-purpose spray adhesive
- Embossing heat gun
- Craft scissors
- Ruler to cut paper squares
- Stamp cleaner and cleaner pad, if desired

1 Before you begin stamping the leaf design onto the cards, start by using a clean and dry stamp to avoid ending up with a different color leaf image than you intended. To get the right amount of ink on the stamp, tap the stamp gently on the ink pad three to five times and then look at the rubber image. If the stamp is correctly inked, you will be able to see the moisture of the ink covering the surface of the image. Repeat with more taps if more ink is needed. Place the stamp straight down onto the paper and push down firmly without rocking or moving the stamp from side to side. Lift the stamp straight up from the paper to avoid distorting the image. Clean the stamp each time a new color is used.

Using the leaf stamp or stamps, press the stamp into the fall-colored ink pad or pads and randomly press the leaf design onto both sides of the 5½-inch-square cards. Some craft stores sell ink pads that contain multiple colors in one pad, which is perfect for this project. However, if a multicolored pad cannot be found, use several colored pads to create different-colored leaves on the front and back sides of the cards.

Clean the rubber stamps to make them last longer. The type of ink pad purchased — such as water-based, dye-based or pigment ink pads — will determine what cleaning method to use. Cleaning solutions can be purchased for hard-to-remove dyes. To remove water-based dyes, clean with a toothbrush and water. Thoroughly dry the rubber stamps before storing them to help them last longer.

2

2 Press a clean leaf stamp into the embossing ink pad. Press the stamp onto the 8½-inch sheets of card stock in several places. Pour the gold embossing powder onto the images. Dump off and then tap off excess powder from the stamped image. Using the heat gun, hold it a few inches away from the embossed leaf. When the image is set, cut it out using the craft scissors.

3

3 Emboss the edges of the 4½-inch and 3½-inch square pieces of card stock. Using the tip of the glue, draw a thin line of glue around the edge of the card and pour the gold embossing powder over the glue. Dump off and then tap off excess powder from the stamped image. Using the heat gun, hold it a few inches away from the embossed leaf.

On the front of the 5½-inch card, glue the 4½-inch square of card stock and top with the 3½-inch square using the glue stick. Cut small pieces of the mounting squares to fit the backs of the cut-out leaves and place the leaves onto the 3½-inch square. Repeat this process on the inside of the card.

If desired, use a script stamp that has personalized wording, such as Thank You, Get Well, Thinking of You or Happy Birthday, on the inside of the card.

Craft Tips

- Homemade cards are great for gift giving. To make these cards to give as gifts, simply tie a few of them with pretty ribbons and they are ready to give.

- Clear plastic sleeves can be purchased at most craft stores that carry stamping supplies to protect the cards for gift giving and keep them looking their best.

- Use these versatile cards as birthday cards, thank you cards, blank note cards, get-well cards or for any occasion imaginable.

- Embossing guns can commonly get as hot as 300°F, so be sure to keep your fingers away from the air when using them. To get the proper ventilation, be sure not to cover the air intake vents with your hands.

FALL BALSAM WREATH

This multipurpose wreath — crafted from fresh balsam branches and assorted colorful fall leaves and berries — will make any room in your home feel like fall. The wreath is simple to make and smells great too … a beautiful embellishment that also fills your home with the aroma of fresh pine.

This easy-to-make wreath uses many tools and supplies probably already found in your home, which makes it cost-effective as well as beautiful. Simple enough, you're embellishing a foam wreath with the essence of the fall harvest. Berries and leaves adorn the wreath, and the natural smell of pine from the balsam branches will leave any room in your home smelling outdoor fresh. The wreath is durable enough to use outdoors as well as indoors, making it functional as well as beautiful.

This project will take approximately 2 hours to complete and cost between $20.00 and $25.00.

1 Cut the balsam branches into one- to 1½-foot pieces. Shave or cut the thicker ends of the branches if necessary to approximately ¼-inch thickness to make them manageable for the staple gun to attach to the foam wreath. Staple the balsam branches to the foam wreath by stapling a single layer of the branches in a circular fashion to the foam wreath to prevent the foam from showing. Staple the branches at the branch end as well as the greenery end to cover the wreath completely.

Materials & Tools

- 14-inch-thick decorative foam wreath ring
- Fresh balsam branches
- Assorted sizes and shapes of fabric or dried fall leaves
- Fabric berries
- 5 yards of 1½-inch-wide wired ribbon (optional)
- Florist wire (optional)
- Wire cutter
- Staple gun
- Hot-glue gun

Craft Tips

- If desired, make a bow using silk ribbon and attach it at the middle of the wreath using florist wire to hold the bow in place at the center. The bow can be created by tying the ribbon into a simple bow shape or by folding a series of loops starting in the center of the ribbon, continuing to create loops until all but approximately six inches of ribbon is left on either side of the loops. Secure the bow by wrapping the bottom of the loops with florist wire.

- Use the wire cutter to cut the thicker ends of the branches into a manageable thickness.

- Use longer staples, such as ½ inch and larger, to attach the branches to the foam wreath. The branches can also be glued using the hot-glue gun to secure them to the wreath.

- Dried leaves can often become very brittle and break. To help preserve them, mix one part glycerin to one part very hot tap water and brush or spray this solution onto the leaves to make them soft and flexible. Let them dry completely before attaching to the garland. Glycerin is a product that is used to soften dry hands and can be purchased over the counter at most pharmacies.

- Balsam branches will last a month or two after cutting without using any preservatives.

2 Staple the branch end of some of the balsam branches on top of the greenery-covered foam wreath. Staple only the branch end to the foam wreath with the greenery facing counterclockwise. Continue stapling branches to the wreath in a counterclockwise fashion until the entire wreath is full and covered.

Using the hot-glue gun, individually glue smaller pieces of the balsam branches to the wreath, overlapping as needed to fill in any spaces or gaps, or place an additional layer of branches on top of the original layer to achieve the desired fullness, filling in empty spaces as necessary.

3 Hot-glue the fall leaves and berries in a circular fashion around the entire wreath on top of the balsam branches. Make a bow using the 5 yards of wired ribbon and florist wire if desired, following the directions in the craft tips.

NATURE'S BOUNTY BASKET

Turn an ordinary basket into a Thanksgiving or fall celebration using autumn elements such as bittersweet, wood, Spanish moss, colorful leaves and acorns.

Use this bountiful basket on an end table, sideboard or hearth. Put fall or Thanksgiving elements such as gourds or apples in the basket for display. Buy an ordinary medium-sized basket or use an old less-than-perfect basket as the base for this project. The basket should have sides with little or no curve to make adhering the elements easier. Gather the natural elements desired from your yard or purchase real or artificial ones in a craft store. You can vary the project's final look depending on elements selected. Use your imagination and be creative!

This project will take approximately 1 hour to complete, depending on size of basket and elements added.

The cost of this project varies greatly. The base cost of the basket can be from $10.00 up, but often an appropriate basket can be found on clearance.

1   Measure side of basket from one handle to the other, for width, and from top of rim to bottom, for height. Trace these measurements on tracing paper or a brown paper bag. Use this area to determine design, number and size of elements needed. When determining the design or layout, create a center focal point with a larger piece of natural material such as bark. The side edges of this space will be under the handle and can be a smaller repeat of the center elements or a continuation of the other elements used. The final elements added will create a focal point at the base of the handle on one side or both sides of the basket.

If using the wood twig discs, cut a few more than needed. Use care in cutting the twigs about ¼ inch thick, as the discs can fly from the saw. Cut the two to four strips of bark to the height measurement of the basket.

Cover work surface with newspaper, as the Spanish moss is very messy. Lay out the elements on paper, with the exception of the Spanish moss. Tip: It is easiest to follow the vertical slats with the design elements. Using glue gun, put glue on one small area at a time and adhere the main elements, such as bark pieces, then the wood discs. The final element to add for the side is the moss. Use enough moss to cover the surface of the basket.

2

3

2 Cut 12 to 15 pieces of florist wire or use twist ties. Drape the bittersweet garland over the handle, attaching it with the wire or ties. Wrap it around the top of the rim. Place wire or ties under the rim, around it and garland, to hold garland in place. Cut garland when it has gone around the rim. Tuck the cut end under garland and wire in place. Make sure ties are twisted securely and cut extra wire. Push any extending sharp wire flat against the basket or handle.

3 Determine on which side of basket to place a focal point at the handle base. Play with elements to be placed here, arranging as desired. Using glue gun, glue the elements in place.

Craft Tips

- When making the wood discs/circles with the miter saw, be very careful, as some pieces may fly from the saw. Wear safety glasses and leather gloves as a precaution.

- Since the outside and handle of the basket will be covered, the condition of the outside surface is not important. The outside of the basket can be spray painted in a dark green or brown to blend better with the elements being added.

MINI-KINDLING BOX

Make this diminutive, decorative but functional kindling box from twigs and cedar board for a rustic, country look. Use it for starter pinecones or twigs, or even a fall dried arrangement for the hearth.

Gather twigs measuring from ½ to ¾ inch in diameter, fairly straight and at least 12½ inches long. Look for ones with decorative elements like knots, moss or birch bark. The kindling box shown measures 12 inches long, 5½ inches wide and 11 inches high. You could increase the length a few inches without changing the other measurements.

This project will take about 1 hour to complete, depending on your sawing skills and equipment available.

The cost is minimal, with the board being the only purchased element, and should be about $4.00. To carry out the rustic look, look for a cedar board that isn't perfect: one with some wear, staining or damage.

Materials & Tools

- 1 (1- by 6- by 3-foot) rough-cut cedar board
- At least 16 feet of twigs ½ to ¾ inch in diameter (more is better, to help choose and cut compatible pieces)
- 4 (1½-inch-long) wood screws
- 24 (at least 1¼-inch-long) nails
- Saw — miter, radial arm or table
- Ruler
- Electric or cordless drill or drill press
- Wood bore bit — ¾ or 1 inch
- Bit — small for nail holes
- Hammer

1 Gather twigs. Cut twelve to fourteen 12½-inch pieces of twig that are relatively straight with saw. Cut one sturdy, slightly curved and decorative twig at least 14 inches long for "handle." Some curve and small knots are okay.

Measure cedar board on smooth side into two 11-inch lengths (sides) and one 10½-inch length (bottom of "box"). Mark and cut with saw. On the two 11-inch boards measure up 5 inches and mark a line across width of board. At the end of the 6-inch length, measure across the end or width and mark the center. It should be at 2¾ inches. Measure ⅜ inch to each side of this mark and mark again. Form and mark the angle by connecting this mark to the 5-inch mark on side of board. Do this on both sides of board. Repeat on other 11-inch board. Cut these pieces following the angled lines.

2 Measure down from narrow part of the side to a width of 2 inches and mark halfway point or center. Drill a ¾-inch hole using the wood bore bit. Drill from both sides to get a smooth hole. Repeat for other side piece. To attach the sides to the bottom, stand sides up against the 10½-inch board with rough-cut side facing out. Working with one side at a time, drill pilot holes at the bottom of side about 1 inch in from side edges and ⅜ inch up from bottom. Insert screws. Repeat for other side.

3 Lay "box" on its side and measure up about 5 inches on each end. At this point start with one of the sturdiest, straightest or most decorative twigs and place across side of "box." Drill a pilot hole about ¾ inch in from each end of twig. Insert nail, and hammer into "box" on each end. Line up next twig. It will take about six 12½-inch twigs on each side, depending on their diameter. If twigs are curved, line up the twigs with curves in the same direction. Last twig should cover the bottom piece of wood. Repeat for other side. If twig for handle does not go into the hole for the handle, whittle a bit of the bark away and insert both ends of "handle." If the handle is loose, wrap raffia around handle and top of side and tie decoratively.

Craft Tip

• Choose the sturdiest and most decorative branch with some curve for the handle.

HALLOWEEN TRICK-OR-TREAT BAG

Make a festive fall bag for trick or treating. These colorful bags are easy to create. Use wool felt for a fun texture.

Celebrate Halloween with your children by making wonderful trick or treat bags for them. This bag is easy to make and fun to create. And the kids will be able to use it through the fall for carrying books from the library or bringing along favorite items on car trips. Wool felt is easy to use because it does not fray. It comes in a wide variety of colors found at the fabric store. Try using other seasonal colors and themes for gifts during any holiday.

This project will take approximately 1 hour and 30 minutes to complete and cost about $20.00.

Materials & Tools

- Black wool felt (two pieces, 13 by 17 inches each)
- Black cotton straps (two pieces, 14 inches long each)
- Brown wool felt (8½ by 11 inches)
- Variety of wool felt in fall colors (5-inch width for cut fabric)
- Variety of embroidery floss matching each of the colors of wool felt
- Double-stick fusible web (pack of five 9- by 12-inch sheets)
- Sewing machine
- Ironing board
- Iron
- Scissors
- Ruler
- Embroidery needle
- Pins
- Black thread
- White chalk

1 First create the bag. Cut two pieces of black wool felt 13- by 17-inches each. With the back sides facing out, sew together the sides and bottom of the bag, leaving a ½-inch seam. Next, face one of the edges of the bag to you and pull apart the front and back of the bag while holding together the bottom of the bag against the flattened sides. Match up the side seam to the bottom seam. From the corner, measure and mark 2 inches on each side using chalk. Take a ruler and draw a line across the two marks. Pin together the material before sewing. Sew the material together using the chalk line as a guide. Repeat on the other side of the bag. This step for sewing the bottom corners will add a nice bucket shape to the bag.

Next, create the top border of the bag. Fold the top down to create a 1-inch border. Pin the fold near the folded edge of the bag. First, sew the cut edge to the bag, leaving a ⅛-inch seam. Then pull the pins out and sew the top edge of the bag, leaving a ⅛-inch seam.

To create handles, cut two cotton straps 14 inches long each. Take one end of a strap and pin it 3 inches from the side of the bag. Make sure the strap is pinned so it can be sewn across twice following the stitch line. Leave about ⅛ inch at the bottom end of the strap. Repeat this with the other end of the strap. Then repeat this step on the other side of the bag with the second strap. Sew the handles to the bag. Remove the pins when finished.

2

3

2 This next step may require a visit to your local specialty paper store. If you do not own a die cutter, you can use one at a specialty paper store for free or for a minimal cost. You could also draw and cut out these shapes by hand. Use a large tree pattern on the brown piece of wool felt. Cut out a variety of fall-colored leaves using a small leaf pattern. For this example, a small maple leaf pattern was used. Repeat this step on the sheets of double-stick fusible web. The fusible web will be used to attach the felt shapes to the bag. Peel off both pieces of backing and apply fusible web to the appropriate shapes.

3 First attach the tree to the front of the bag. Next put some leaves on the branches of the tree. Then apply some leaves falling off the tree and a few on the ground. Iron the shapes permanently onto the bag.

Finally, hand-stitch vein lines onto each leaf. Mix and match different-colored embroidery floss to different-colored leaves. For example, use orange thread on a red leaf and use red thread on an orange leaf. This will create more interest while still creating a color-coordinated piece.

Craft Tip

- Visit your local specialty paper store to use a die cutter for the tree and leaf shapes. Or draw and cut out these shapes by hand.

SCARECROW WALL HANGING

For centuries, scarecrows have frightened critters away from family gardens and farm crops.
By definition, scarecrows frighten without causing harm. So although scarecrows may spook
some animals, in actuality they are harmless, and so being are truly good-natured.

The scarecrow is a throwback to a time before the industrial revolution and factory farming — a time when families would sow the earth by hand, living in harmony with nature. Today many small family farms have been replaced by factory farms, leaving far fewer scarecrows to decorate the landscape. This scarecrow decorative wall hanging pays homage to a simpler time when man was part of nature, rather than just living nearby.

This project will take approximately 1 hour to complete and cost about $25.00.

Materials & Tools

- Pre-sewn stuffable 12-inch muslin doll body
- 1 cup of cold coffee
- 1 ounce of polyester fiberfill
- Doll-sized overalls for 12-inch doll
- Doll-sized flannel shirt for 12-inch doll
- Doll farmer's hat for 12-inch doll
- 1- by 1-inch piece of flannel fabric
- 2- by 2-inch piece of black felt
- 2- by 2-inch piece of orange felt
- Curly raffia or hay (approximately 30 pieces, 12 inches each)
- 6 inches brown embroidery floss
- 5-inch wooden dowel, ¼-inch diameter
- Needle
- Tacky glue
- Hair dryer

Craft Tip

- Recycle; use old doll clothes to make your scarecrow. Instead of using a wooden dowel, try cutting down a disposable chopstick!

1 The first step is to prepare the doll's body. Use a 12-inch pre-sewn stuffable muslin doll body for the base of your scarecrow. Purchase these at most arts and crafts stores. If you are reusing old doll clothes from a larger or smaller doll, purchase an appropriately sized stuffable doll.

To begin, prepare the doll. Soak the muslin in regular strength coffee. This will give the muslin an old-world, more worn-out look. After evenly soaking the muslin, squeeze out as much moisture as possible and then finish drying the fabric with a hair dryer.

Before stuffing the doll, stitch a smile on the doll's face with embroidery floss. The mouth should be imperfectly shaped so as to be more like an actual scarecrow. Yet however imperfectly sewn the mouth is, be sure to make it a smile; we're trying to scare crows, not kids! Once the mouth has been stitched on the doll, you can fill it with fiberfill. Stuff only the body, head, hands and lower arms of the doll. Do not stuff the doll's upper arms or legs, as we will deal with these areas later in the project.

When your doll is stuffed, put the finishing touches on its face. Using a small piece of black felt, cut small circle shapes to be used for eyes. If you are using a twelve-inch doll, the circles should be just shy of ¼ inch. Affix these circles to the doll's face using tacky glue. Then cut a small triangle from your orange felt and affix it to the doll's face in place of the nose. Try putting the triangle on slightly askew for a more realistic feel.

2 Dress the muslin scarecrow. The best outfit for a scarecrow is overalls with a flannel patch. Don't worry if they're old or tattered; the more worn, the better! We'll start with the overalls. Carefully cut the lower legs of the overalls. Cut only enough to begin the process of fraying the fabric, about ⅛ inch up. After cutting the legs, use a needle to fray the denim. Create approximately ⅛ inch of fray at the base of the overalls.

Now take your 1- by 1-inch piece of flannel and sew it to the knee of the overalls. This piece will look like a fabric patch used to mend a hole.

Remember, this is one project where it's okay to do rough sewing work: the rougher, the better. With your needle, fray the edges of the patch as well, the same way you frayed the denim. Place the muslin doll in the denim overalls.

3 Embellish your scarecrow. For legs, stuff the denim overall legs with hay or curly raffia. Bunch approximately 20 pieces of foot-long hay together and fold them in half. Once folded, wrap a small piece of string around the center of the folded hay, and tie into a knot. When the knot has been tied, stuff the hay in the first pants leg as far as it will go. Cut off any excess hay that sticks out of the overalls more than 1 inch. Repeat this process for the second leg.

No scarecrow is complete without a straw hat. To liven up your scarecrow, try adding a sunflower button to the straw hat. Affix the button to the front of the straw hat using a needle and thread. Finally, place the 5-inch wooden dowel across the back of the doll; poke one end into each arm. Ideally, the scarecrow's arms should hang from the dowels and dangle.

WIRE LUMINARIA

Decorative flair shines through in this lighting project that is both easy to create and beautiful to behold. Let it light up your autumn nights!

A lit candle crafted in twisted copper wire can be made to hang anywhere a decorating accent of light will enhance your home decor. Using thin-gauge copper wire, you can twist and shape a lighting accent into any desired design to hold a votive candle. Twist beads into the wire design to add extra color. Decorative beads of leaves, flowers or snowflakes can change the design for each season.

This project will take approximately 45 minutes to complete and cost about $7.00.

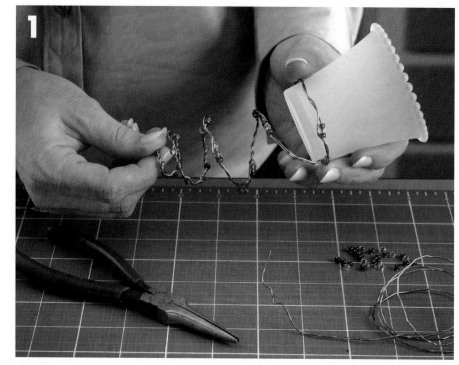

1 Measure a 20-inch length of wire to make supportive base for the votive candle. Cut two pieces. Taking flat-nosed pliers, hold both wires together and twist lengths together. As you twist, add beads for color, one on a piece, using the second wire to twist around and hold the bead in place. When wire and beads are twisted together to the end, take round-nosed pliers and loop ends to finish. Make sure ends are twisted into a circle to avoid sharp ends. Make the finished twisted wire circle the base of the votive candle, making a cradle to hold the candle in place. Twist wire together. Extra wire length can now be twisted below the candle base into a spiral shape.

Materials & Tools

- 10 yards of 20-gauge copper wire
- Glass candle votive
- Colored glass beads
- Decorative beads for seasonal use
- Rubber band
- Wire cutters
- Flat-nosed pliers
- Round-nosed pliers

Craft Tips

- Make sure beads are big enough to thread onto wire.
- Add charms to add interest.
- Look for a variety of votive candles in shapes and colors to interchange to fit a mood or season. Decorative accents of dried flowers or leaves can also be twisted into the wire form.
- Fill the votive with water to use as a hanging floral vase.

2 Measure height of glass votive, adding extra length for decorative twists and loops. Cut eight pieces of wire to this measure. Using flat-nosed pliers, hold two wires together at the top and begin twisting wires, adding beads along the way as in Step 1. Continue this process to make four twisted sections of wire and beads. Taking the wire base completed in Step 1, measure four equal sections and attach each of the four new wires to each section by using the round-nosed pliers to loop, twist and tighten. Take each wire section up to top of the glass votive, form into desired shape, twisting and looping wire. Use rubber band to hold the four sections in place.

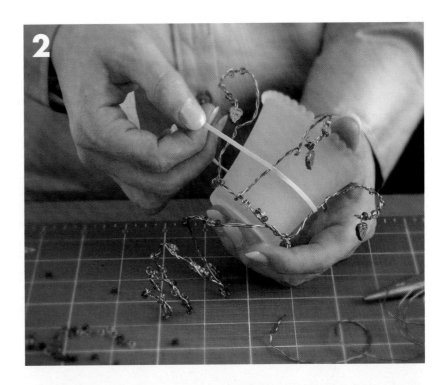

3 The final hanger can be measured to any preferred length for hanging. Add to this measure an amount of wire to wrap around the votive where the rubber band is positioned. Measure two pieces of wire, cut and use flat-nosed pliers to hold and twist into a shape. Again, beads or other decorative charms can be added. Wrap wire around votive where rubber band is placed. Secure one end, leaving excess wire to be drawn up into the hanger. Take each of the four sections and loop them through this tightened circle to secure holder in place. Cut off rubber band. Take remaining end of wire and loop over the top of the votive to form hanger. Extra beads or charms can be added by taking pieces of wire and adding them to the hanger design. Secure the other end of the hanger to the top circle of the glass votive. Reshape any wire at base or sides that may have been shifted during the construction.

Experiment with changing the shape of loops and swirls until the desired effect is reached. Place candle in finished glass votive and light up your world with this wire-designed luminaria.

FALL LEAF CLAY POT

The centerpiece for your table sets the visual mood, whether it's elegant or earthy. In autumn, leaves are a colorful and natural choice when creating a centerpiece.

The surface of your dining room table is like a blank canvas, just waiting for you to paint. You can create many "pictures," starting with your tablecloth, napkins and dishes. The best and most important way to complete the look is to add a special centerpiece that draws it all together. This project is a simple one to do, yet the results are rich and dramatic.

This project will take approximately 30 to 45 minutes to complete, not including drying time between steps, and cost about $12.00.

Materials & Tools

- Large plastic or clay pot (shown is an 8-inch plastic pot)
- Acrylic paints: yellow, brown and red
- Photocopies of fall leaves (or Photo Images (fall leaves) found in craft and scrapbooking stores)
- Mod Podge (found in the glue section of a craft store)
- Crackle medium (found in the paint section of a craft store)
- Paintbrush
- Scissors
- Sea sponge (optional)

1 Paint the plastic or clay pot with two coats of yellow paint and let it dry completely. Paint the rim of the pot red. Gather some beautifully colored fall leaves and make photocopies of them, enough to encircle the pot. Cut them out.

2 Brush one smooth coat of crackle medium on the painted yellow surface, and then follow the manufacturer's directions. Most products say to let the crackle medium become tacky, but not dry, before painting on the top coat. You can brush on the brown paint with a paintbrush or a sponge. Let this dry completely. Repeat this process with the rim of the pot, applying the crackle medium, and then, again following the manufacturer's directions, paint the yellow paint over the red rim.

3 With a paintbrush, apply a moderate amount of Mod Podge around the middle of the pot and place the leaves where desired. Smooth out any air bubbles on the leaves, and then apply Mod Podge over the leaves as well. When this is dry, paint the entire pot and rim with Mod Podge, because this product is also a sealer.

Craft Tips

- To experiment with the crackle finish, paint small sections INSIDE the pot, and then "crackle" them to see which effect you like. You will get different effects by adding heavier or lighter paint and using a sponge as opposed to a brush.
- Fill the decorated pot with mums or fresh flowers from your garden, placing them in a vase no taller than the clay pot, and add Spanish moss around the edges to fill in. Or you may choose to buy artificial mums, flowers or ivy, or simply fill it with branches with fall leaves that you find outside — maybe the very leaves that inspired your project.

RED TWIG DOGWOOD BUSH

After all the leaves have fallen, the red twig dogwood is one of the yard's (and nature's) most attractive ornamental shrubs. But it's not just an outdoor decoration. Now you can bring it indoors to fill an empty corner in your home. Decorate the branches for fall, but don't stop there. Change the decorations for other holidays that follow.

Combine your fall yard chores with a fall craft project. Cut long branches from red twig dogwood bushes that need to be pruned. Arrange them in a sand-filled pottery vase or crock. Add a small bird nest, birds and birdhouses or other fall decorations, or leave the branches unadorned for a more rustic look. The branches will add height and interest to any empty corner.

This project will take approximately 1 hour to complete and cost about $25.00.

Materials & Tools

- Red twig dogwood branches
- Sand or small aquarium rocks
- Pottery vase or crock
- Twine or raffia
- Optional decorations
- Pruning shears or clipper

1 Cut six to eight branches about 5 to 6 feet long from a red twig dogwood shrub.

2 Trim the branches as needed and arrange them in a pottery vase or crock. Hold the

arrangement in place by tying it with about two feet of twine about six inches from the top of the vase or crock. Pour aquarium rock or sand into the vase and cover the branches to hold them in place and weight the bottom of the vase.

3 Purchase or make small ornaments to hang on the branches. Vary the ornaments depending upon the season. Fall decorations include ornamental birds, nests or birdhouses. Small baskets are also fun to hang on the branches.

F A L L

DECORATING

The colors of fall — which range from the season's bright leaves of orange, red, yellow and burgundy to subtler undertones of russet, tan, gray and brown — present wonderful opportunities for decorating your home. So do the season's many textures. We combine it all here in this chapter full of autumn decorating projects. Put them to good use as you celebrate the beauty of our most changeable season.

Facing page: Witch Mobile, page 100

ANTIQUE POTPOURRI JAR

Antique jars look great filled with potpourri. Add a family memory for a special touch! Compose a small verse noting a special family memory, and scribe the verse in hand-printed calligraphy or print it with a computer in a signature script on a small card. Trim the card with ribbon and gold-tinted marker.

Dried flowers are fragile and tend to break off as they are separated for most craft projects. Collect the small remnants of flowers and leaves in an open pan or bowl as the projects are progressing. After all the other projects are done, use the remnants for potpourri! Add a little scent to the dried flowers and place them in your antique jar for display. The bright colors of all the broken flowers add flair to any shelf or bookcase where the jars are displayed. The memory card inside makes it a great gift to give to family members as a special remembrance of days gone by.

This project will take approximately 2 hours to complete and will cost about $20.00.

Materials & Tools

- Potpourri
- Scent or fragrance
- Antique jars with wire bale
- Card stock
- Calligraphy pen or computer and printer
- Ribbon
- Gold-tinted felt-tip marker
- Torn cloth strip
- Paper trimmer or cutter
- Corner paper punch
- Hole paper punch
- Spatula
- Shallow pan

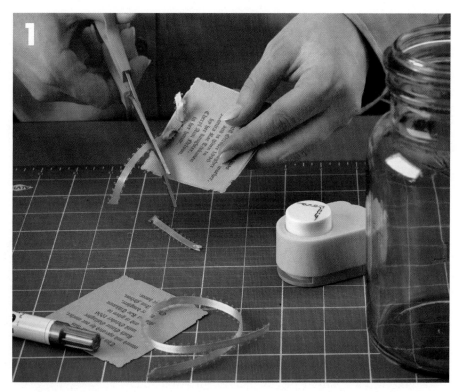

1 Wash and dry the antique jar until it shines. Select a card stock in a color that complements the flowers in the potpourri. If using a calligraphy pen, cut the card stock into 3- by 3-inch squares and print the family memory verse on the cards. If using a computer to print, use a word processing program and the insert table function to divide the card into equal sections. Type the memory into the sections and print in a font size, color and style to match the card stock color. Cut the printed card stock into 3- by 3-inch squares. Use a paper punch to shape or trim the corners. Using a gold-tinted marker, place an even edge of gold around all four sides of the card. Using a paper punch, punch two small holes near the top or bottom of the verse. Poke each end of a color-matched ribbon through the two holes on the printed side of the card. Cross over the ribbon on the back of the paper and poke the ends through the two holes again so that they are on the printed side of the card again. Do not cross over again, but poke the ribbon ends back down into the two holes, leaving a small section of ribbon above the hole to look like the loops of a ribbon. Cross the ends over again and poke them through the holes one last time to form the streamers on the bow. Trim the ends as needed.

2 Collect the remnants of flowers in an open pan or bowl. Discard the stems and keep the most colorful parts of the flowers and leaves. Put the broken parts in a colander with large holes to shake out the small pieces or any dirt that may have been collected with the flower remnants. Add a drop or two of scent or fragrance.

3 Place card in jar so that verse can be seen through the glass. Hold the card in place against the glass with a spatula while filling the jar with potpourri prepared in Step 2. Close the cover and tie a piece of color-coordinated cloth ribbon on the wire bale.

Craft Tips

- The special part of this craft is developing a verse for the family memory. Include family names and dates to make them more specific. Create a memory capsule for each member of your family.

- The flowers will lose their color in time, but the memory will not fade. Change the flowers each year to keep the jar looking fresh. If the card needs to be freshened up, use the instructions above to create a new one.

- The antique jar was used for canning in days gone by and was a valued tool for most of our mothers and grandmothers. The phrase "owned and operated by" is a great way to describe the purpose of the jar in the family memory. The jar can be handed down for generations to come and valued because you remember its original owner and operator.

BIRDHOUSE SHOE RACK

Tripping over shoes in the front entry can be a thing of the past with this useful birdhouse shoe rack to shelve the whole family's shoes. You can remove the shelves for easy clean up, and washable paint makes the job even easier.

How many times have you wished you had a place to put all the shoes that pile up by the door of your busy family's home? This decorative and useful shoe rack adds charm to your home decor and also serves as a place to stack all the family shoes in one neat and convenient place. You can also use it in your closet to organize the shoes that you don't wear every day. For larger closets, make two racks for his-and-her shoe collections.

This project takes about 2 days to create, allowing time for the paint to dry. To cut the project out of wood takes about 4 hours. To paint the project takes about 2 hours, and the final assembly after all the paint dries is less than an hour.

The cost of this project is approximately $25.00.

Materials & Tools

- One 1- by 12-inch, 4-foot pine board
- Three 1- by 4-inch, 6-foot pine boards
- One 1- by 6-inch, 6-foot pine board
- Finishing nails
- Wood glue
- Washable interior paint
- Craft paint for accent color
- One ½-inch-square wooden dowel
- Four ½-inch-round wooden dowels
- Pencil
- Wood putty
- Paintbrushes
- Handsaw or table saw
- Hammer or nail gun
- Power drill
- 1-inch hole saw bit
- ½-inch drill bit

1 CUTTING THE WOOD PIECES

Birdhouse end pieces: Cut the ends of the birdhouse shoe rack using the 1- by 12-inch pine board. The board will actually measure about 11¼ inches wide. On the outside edges, measure and draw a horizontal mark 16 inches from one end of the board on each side of the board. Draw a lengthwise line down the center of the board. On the centerline of the board, measure and draw a mark 21½ inches from the end of the board. Draw a line from each of the 16-inch marks to the 21½-inch mark to form the top of the roofline of the birdhouse. Continue to draw the line all the way to either side of the board to create the peak for both sides of the rack at the same time. Cut on this line with a table saw or handsaw to create the peak of each birdhouse end piece.

On the centerline of each of the end pieces, measure and draw horizontal marks 8½ inches from the bottom end of the end piece and 16 inches from the bottom end of the end piece. Using a 1-inch hole saw bit, drill a hole where the horizontal marks intersect the centerline to create the bird hole entrance to the birdhouse. Make sure the hole is drilled through the entire thickness of the board.

Now align the two boards so they face each other. Open the facing pieces like a book. On the

inside of each of the end pieces, measure and mark a line 1⅞ inches from the back of the end piece and another line 5¼ inches from the back of the end piece. On the 1⅞-inch line, draw intersecting horizontal mark 2½ inches and 11½ inches from the bottom of the end piece. On the 5¼-inch line, draw an intersecting horizontal mark ⅞ inch and 10 inches from the bottom of the end piece. Using the ½-drill bit, drill a hole on each of the four intersecting marks but do NOT drill all the way through the board. These holes will be used to place the wooden dowels, which connect the end pieces.

Rails for front and back rack: Using two of the 6-foot, 1- by 4-inch boards, measure, mark and cut four 28-inch lengths from the board. Using three of these 28-inch boards, cut each board in half lengthwise to form six rails measuring about 1¾ inches by 28 inches. (You will only need five of these for the project.)

Shelf backs: From the fourth 28-inch piece, cut about ¼ inch from one end so that it measures 27¾ inches. Cut this piece in three equal pieces lengthwise to form three pieces measuring 1¼ inches by 27¾ inches. These will be used to nail

to the back of the shelf to create the back hanging edge of each shelf. (You will only need two of these for the project.)

Shelves: Using the 6-foot, 1- by 6-inch board, measure, mark and cut two 27¾-inch pieces to be used for the shelf pieces.

Dowels: Measure, mark and cut all four dowels at 29 inches.

Roof: From the scraps of wood from the 1 by 4 boards not used in the rail pieces (1¾-inch-wide rail), measure, mark and cut two 9-inch pieces and two 9¾-inch pieces. (Final dimensions will be 1¾ inches by 9 inches and 1¾ inches by 9¾ inches.)

Perch: From the ½-inch-square dowel, cut four 2-inch pieces to place under the bird entrance hole for the bird perch.

2 ASSEMBLING THE BIRDHOUSE RACK

Placing wooden dowel: Put four 29-inch wooden dowels in each of the eight predrilled holes on the inside of the end pieces. You may glue in place or leave free, based on your own preference. Once the 29-inch dowels are in place inside the predrilled holes, a 28-inch opening will be available to place between the front and back rails.

Placing rails: Put a bead of wood glue on the end of each rail before nailing. Place a rail piece on the front and back bottom of the inside of each of the birdhouse end pieces. Using a nail gun, nail the rail in place by placing a nail on the outside of the end piece through the rail. A hand drill may also be used to predrill a nail hole, and then a hammer and nail can be used to attach the rails to the end piece. Placement of the two bottom rail pieces stabilizes the ends so that the upper rails can now be installed. There are three rails in the back and two rails in the front of the end pieces.

On the back of the inside of both end pieces, measure and mark a horizontal mark 9 inches from the bottom of the end piece. Place the bottom edge of the rail at the 9-inch mark and nail on each side using a nail gun or drill, hammer and nails. Place the top edge of a rail at the top back of each end piece just under the cut angle of the roof peak. Nail in place with a nail gun or drill, hammer and nail.

Measure and make a horizontal mark 8 inches from the bottom on the front of the end piece. Place the bottom edge of the rail at the 8-inch mark and nail on each side using a nail gun or drill, hammer and nails.

Assembling shelves: Add a bead of wood glue to the shelf back. Using a nail gun or drill, hammer and nails, nail the shelf back to the shelf. The back will hang a little below the shelf to create a hanger when the shelf is placed on the dowels.

Fill all nail holes with wood putty and allow to dry. The end pieces, rails, dowels and shelves can now be painted with a washable interior paint.

3   FINAL PAINTING AND ASSEMBLY

Assembling roof and perches: Paint the roof and perch pieces using a complementary craft paint that matches your home decor. Wait until the paint is dry on the roof and perch pieces and the rest of the shelving unit. Put a bead of wood glue on the top edge of each end piece. Being careful not to smear the wood glue, line up the 9-inch roof piece with the top peak of the roofline on the end piece. Make sure that the lengthwise side of it hangs over the outside edge of the end piece to resemble an overhang on a roofline. Nail the roof piece in place with the nail gun or drill, hammer and nails. Repeat on the other end piece. With the 9¾-inch roof piece, align the second roof piece with the top edge of the first roof piece. Nail in place with a nail gun or drill, hammer and nails. Repeat on the other end piece.

Measure and make a horizontal mark 1 inch below the center of each bird hole entrance. Hammer a nail partially through the center of each perch piece. (Option: Add a drop of wood glue to the back of the perch piece.) Center a perch piece under each bird hole entrance on the 1-inch mark and tap the partially hammered nail on the perch in place on the end piece. Fill nail holes with wood putty and allow to dry. Touch up the nail holes with craft paint.

Installing shelf: After all pieces are dry, the top shelf can be hung in place by placing the back edge of the shelf over the top back dowel and allowing the front edge of the shelf to rest on the top front dowel. The second shelf can be installed by putting the back edge of a shelf over the bottom back dowel and allowing the front edge of the shelf to rest on the bottom front dowel. Remove shelves as needed for easy cleaning.

FRAMED AND PRESSED FALL-COLORED LEAVES

Enjoy the fabulous colors of fall throughout the year when you frame pressed leaves in a decorative frame with colorful backgrounds that complement the leaf colors. Select leaves that match your wallpaper or other home decorations to carry your leaf theme statement throughout your home.

Leaf colors and shapes are a popular theme in many natural wall paints and papers. Gather the bounty of fall leaves from your yard, press them and then use the pressed leaves to decorate artistic frames. The shape and detail of fall leaves can not be duplicated easily, so use the exquisite detail of the real thing instead of trying to recreate it with paint or other mediums.

This project will take approximately 30 minutes to complete and cost about $15.00.

Materials & Tools

- Air-dry or microwave press
- Paper trimmer
- Colored card stock
- Complementary-colored, precut mat
- Decorative frames
- Pressed leaves
- Double-backed tape or tabs
- Glass cleaner
- Paper towels

1 Find and select fall-colored leaves from your yard. Try to select them before they fall to the ground to ensure the freshest-looking leaves. Select many different colors, sizes and shapes. Oak and maple leaves have the most variety of colors, but many other types of leaves will also do. Press the leaves using a microwave flower press. You can also use an air-dry press, but the microwave press is faster and will give you instant results. You will know how the leaves look within a few minutes so you will have time to select more leaves if you don't like the way yours turned out. The microwave press comes with two square terra cotta presses, two felt pads and two muslin liners. Place one press inside up on the counter. Press a felt pad squarely over it, followed by a muslin liner. Arrange three to four fresh leaves on the liner and slightly flatten with your fingers. Place the second muslin liner over the leaves, followed by the second felt pad and second press, this time inside down. Place a large rubber band around the press. Ensure all the parts are square with each other and no part of the leaf is sticking out of the press. Place the press in the microwave and microwave at high for 1 minute. If needed, turn the press and microwave for another minute. You may have to experiment with the correct amount of time by testing several leaves, but it typically only takes 1 to 2 minutes for each batch of three to four leaves. Open the press to check the leaves. They should be flat and slightly crisp to the touch. Take each leaf out of the press and arrange them on a paper towel in a flat box. Layer with additional paper towels if doing several leaves at a time, and set aside until you are ready to use them.

2 Take the purchased frame apart and clean the glass on both sides with glass cleaner and a paper towel. Experiment with different colors, sizes and shapes of leaves by laying them out on different colors of card stock and then placing the mat over them. Try different arrangements until you find the one you want. Try tearing the card stock into different shapes and layering the colors for different effects. Once you find the arrangement you like, you are ready for the assembly.

3 Select the card stocks you want to use. Trim the outside dimensions of the background color so that it fits in the frame. Tear complementary colors in sizes that are small enough to fit inside the mat. Arrange the torn pieces and the leaves on the background paper until it suits you. Put the mat on top to ensure you like the arrangement. Remove the mat and put double-backed tape or tabs under the torn card stock or leaves to ensure that it stays in the position you like. Replace the mat. It's fun to place the leaves so that a little edge of the leaves will peak out from under the mat. Cover the mat with the glass, being careful not to get fingerprints on it. Place the frame face down on the counter. Carefully flip the glass and other layers over and place in the frame. Check out the arrangement to ensure there was no slippage of the arrangement. Place the back of the frame over the layers and close according to manufacturer's instructions. Make two or three frames and hang them together in an arrangement on an empty wall.

Craft Tips

- This project is so easy, you will want to do it over and over again to give as a gift. Change the color of the card stock, the frame and the leaves to match your friend or family's décor so that your gift is personalized just for them.

- Each year, you can replace last year's leaves and make new arrangements. You can also press leaves in the spring or summer to add to your fall-colored leaves. Combining the colors from spring, summer and fall in one frame can give you the impression of several seasons at a glance.

FALL GUEST HAND TOWEL

It's fun to have fall-colored finger towels in your kitchen or bathroom, but not always possible to find the right size or color to match your decor. So use "fat quarters" in multiple matching colors or prints to create several coordinating towels. To add a fall theme, use pressed leaves from your yard to create a pattern for a leaf applique.

Most people who sew or quilt are familiar with the fat quarters sold in fabric stores. Many stores also group several complementary colors of fat quarters together in a bunch to be used for quilting projects which require multiple matching colors. Select several of the pieces from a bunch and use them to make the perfect size finger towel. It's getting harder to find small finger towels to hang on your smaller decorative racks, but this is a great way to make the towel just the size you need. To add detail, stamp and stitch a picture on the leaf before it is appliqued to the towel.

This project will take approximately 4 hours to complete and cost about $12.00.

Materials & Tools

- Pressed fall leaf
- Card stock
- Pencil
- Heatnbond fusible fabric
- Several pieces of fall-colored fat quarters
- Thread
- Embroidery floss
- Scissors
- Needles
- Sewing machine
- Fall-theme stamp(s)
- Washable stamping ink pad
- Iron
- Air-dry or microwave flower press

1 Wash, dry and press the fat quarters. Fold the bottom edge over ¼ inch and press. Fold again and press to create a finished edge. With a sewing machine, sew the pressed edge using a ¼-inch seam allowance. Fold, press and sew one side of the fabric at a time, starting with the bottom edge and then moving to the top edge, left edge and right edge.

2 Press several different sizes, colors and types of leaves according to the manufacturer's directions for your type of press. Trace the outside edge of the leaf on a piece of card stock using a pencil to make a pattern piece. Using the pattern piece, trace the leaf pattern onto the paper side of the Heatnbond with a pencil. Repeat the tracing to make the appropriate number of leaves intended for the project. Cut out the pattern from the Heatnbond, leaving a ¼-inch allowance all around. Press the pattern piece, paper side up, onto the wrong side of a leaf-colored fabric. Cut out the pattern by cutting on the pencil lines. Stamp a fall-theme stamp in the center of the leaf cutout on the fabric side using a washable stamping ink pad. Remove the paper back from the back of the fabric leaf piece. With embroidery floss, stitch the outline of the stamp using a backstitch, satin stitch or French knot as needed.

3 Arrange one to three leaves on the bottom third of the hand towel. Put the hand-stitched leaf in the center of the leaves if more than one leaf is used. Using a hot iron, press the leaves onto the finger towel. With embroidery floss, stitch the outer edge of each leaf, using the blanket stitch. Using a backstitch, stitch the outline of the veins in the leaf. Wash and press the hand towel to remove stamping ink and wrinkles. Hang on a small decorative rail. Enjoy!

Craft Tips

- Other towels can also be used, even though they come in larger sizes. Purchase plaid kitchen hand towels and appliqué a larger leaf pattern. Use cotton terry cloth hand towels for a fun bathroom hand towel. Use lighter colored towels so that the leaf pattern is apparent.

- As the seasons change, vary the color of the towel and the type of applique to match the season.

- To attach the towel to a drawer knob or handle, tear a strip of coordinating fabric about 2 inches wide and 8 or 9 inches long. Remove loose threads to make a frayed edge. Fold the towel in thirds the long way. Tie the strip of fabric around the upper third of the towel tightly. Fold the towel down at the tie, with the shorter end of the towel to the back. Tie on to the handle or knob. Smooth out the fabric tie to resemble a small tie bow.

DRIED APPLE GARLAND

This multipurpose apple garland, crafted from dehydrated apples, makes a beautiful fall adornment for the home. Apples from the fall harvest are dehydrated and hot-glued to a pine rope garland, creating a stunning work of art to decorate a fireplace mantel, hang over a door or window, or act as a tabletop centerpiece.

Whoever said not to play with your food? This impressive and showy decoration lets you do just that by creating a work of art from freshly picked apples from the fall harvest. There are many methods to dehydrate fruit; this technique is easy and cost-effective, and the end result will leave you feeling completely satisfied. Slowly dehydrate the apples in the oven using low heat and the simple element of time. While the apples are dehydrating, you can easily complete the remainder of the wreath using supplies found at most craft stores.

This project will take approximately 12 hours to complete and cost about $20.00 to $25.00.

1 Heat oven to 195°F. When choosing which apples to purchase for the garland, you may choose any variety of colored apples. You may choose to use the apples you have on hand or mix and match colors for different and unique results. Any ripe but firm apple with no blemishes or bruises will work well for dehydrating.

Using a chef's knife, slice the apples into horizontal ⅛-inch- to ¼-inch-thick slices to expose the apple's star shape in the center. Place lemon juice in medium-sized bowl and dip the apples in the lemon juice to prevent them from turning brown.

Generously spray the baking racks with nonstick cooking spray to prevent the apples from sticking during the baking process. Place the apple slices onto the sprayed wire baking racks and place the racks on baking sheets. Bake 3 to 4 hours at 195°F. Several racks of apples can be baked at the same time. Rotate the racks once during baking time. Turn the oven off and leave the apples in the oven with the door closed for 6 to 8 hours or overnight. Do not open the oven door because the remaining heat is needed to slowly dehydrate the apple slices.

Materials & Tools

- 2 to 3 pounds assorted apples, such as Red Delicious or Granny Smith
- 1 cup lemon juice
- Nonstick cooking spray
- All-purpose spray varnish
- Pine rope-style garland, approximately 3 feet long
- Fabric or dried fall leaves, such as maple
- Mini plastic apple ornaments
- 5 yards 1½-inch-wide wired ribbon
- Florist wire
- Chef's knife
- Wire baking racks
- Baking sheets
- Hot-glue gun

2 Remove the sliced apples from the wire baking racks and place them on a piece of disposable cardboard; spray both sides of the apple slices with varnish, following the manufacturer's instructions. Be sure to use the varnish in a well-ventilated area or outdoors.

Using the hot-glue gun, individually glue the apple slices to the garland, overlapping as needed to fill the space on the garland. Fill in empty spaces with more of the apple slices, or place an additional layer of apples on top of the original layer to achieve the desired fullness of the garland. Hot-glue the leaves and mini apples intermittently to the garland in between the dried apples to the desired fullness.

3 Make a bow using the silk ribbon and attach it at the middle of the garland using florist wire to hold the bow in place at the center. To create the bow, tie the ribbon into a simple bow shape or fold a series of loops starting in the center of the ribbon, continuing to create loops until all but approximately six inches of ribbon is left on either side of the loops. To secure the bow, wrap the bottom of the loops with florist wire.

Craft Tips

- Dehydrate the apples using a purchased commercial dehydrator; follow the manufacturer's instruction manual for specific details on how to dehydrate apples.

- Dried leaves can often become very brittle and break. To help preserve them, mix one part glycerin to one part very hot tap water and brush or spray this solution onto the leaves to make them soft and flexible. Let them dry completely before attaching to the garland. Glycerin is a product that is used to soften dry hands; you can purchase it over the counter at most pharmacies.

- To personalize the garland, add different embellishments such as fall flowers, leaves, nuts or other fruit.

- Most of the items (spray varnish, rope garland, ribbon, florist wire, mini apples and glue) are available at any craft store.

- To double the length of this garland, buy a longer piece of rope garland and double the amount of dehydrated apples, leaves and mini apples called for in the instructions.

- To save time, make the ribbon and hot-glue the leaves and mini apples to the garland while waiting for apples to dehydrate.

- If you omit mini apples, add more dehydrated apple slices in their place.

- If you can't find rope garland in three-foot lengths, simply fold longer pieces of rope garland in half or in thirds to create the length needed.

Pumpkin Container with Mum Plant

Turn an artificial or real pumpkin into a container for a lovely potted fall plant.

Embellished with fall elements such as leaves, artificial gourds or bittersweet/fall garland and finished with a wired bow in fall colors, this is a great indoor decorating piece for table or hearth. Use an artificial or real mum plant for indoors. If using a real mum plant, put a saucer inside the pumpkin under the pot to contain excess water.

When making this project for outdoors, use a real pumpkin and real mum plant. Add elements that can withstand the outdoors — gourds, colored corn, leaves or corn husks. Finish everything off with a raffia bow. Make a few of these pumpkin containers in varying sizes for the front steps. To attach the gourds, use wooden florist picks or skewers; for the other elements, use raffia. Don't forget to save the pumpkin seeds and roast them for a tasty fall treat.

This project will take less than 1 hour to complete.

Cost will vary. Using all artificial elements, the cost at full retail can be about $30.00; however, often these elements are substantially discounted well before the season. When making the outdoor version, in season, the real elements are inexpensive.

Materials & Tools

- Pumpkin — artificial (foam or papier-mâché) or real
- Mum plant — artificial or real
- Fall leaves — artificial or real in a few colors to enhance the mum plant
- Wired ribbon in fall colors — about 60 inches — or raffia for outdoors
- Other fall elements, as desired
- Florist or "U" pins — a few
- Florist wire or florist tape (optional)
- Wooden skewers or wooden florist picks if using real gourds — a few
- Tracing paper or brown paper bag
- Felt-tipped marker
- Serrated paring knife

1 Measure the top of the pot and trace a circle slightly less than that size on tracing paper or a brown paper bag. Cut out the pattern and center it on top of the pumpkin and trace with a felt-tipped marker. Cut out top of pumpkin with a serrated knife.

2

3

2 Check size of hole by placing the pot into the pumpkin. The fit should be a bit tight, so the pot does not drop all the way into the pumpkin. Having the rim of the pot extending a bit above the pumpkin helps in adding the elements, such as the ribbon. If the hole is too large and the pot drops too low into the pumpkin, add elements such as marbles or rocks in the bottom of the pumpkin to hold the pot higher. Remember, if it is a real mum, place a saucer in the bottom of the pumpkin to contain any excess water. When pot fits appropriately into pumpkin, it is ready to decorate.

3 For the indoor version of this project, work with the leaves or any other appropriate fall floral elements, placing them around the base of the mum plant. When happy with the arrangement, use florist pins to hold the decorative elements in place. It may be easiest to make the leaves into a garland first and then wrap it around, securing with florist pins. Make the garland using either florist wire or florist tape. When finished with these elements or any additional desired, place the ribbon around the rim of pot and tie in front of pumpkin. If making the outdoor version, put wooden skewers or wooden florist picks into the gourds and place other end of pick into the pumpkin, slightly outside the rim of the pot. Use leaves and/or corn husks as in the artificial version. Use raffia around the rim and tie a bow or tie colored corn to this instead of a bow.

Craft Tips

- If using a real pumpkin, place it outdoors and embellish accordingly. Use a foam or papier-mâché pumpkin for indoors, according to the instructions below.
- When making the artificial or real pumpkin container, purchase a pumpkin large enough to hold the mum pot, leaving a few inches of pumpkin all the way around it.

WITCH MOBILE

Give this Halloween mobile a look as elaborate or as spooky as you wish.

This project starts with a quarter moon as the focal point and features a witch silhouette, bats, beads and marbles as well. Make it with or without a votive candle holder.

Use a sheet of craft copper and Halloween-shaped metal cutouts, such as bats, to create the mobile. Use leather gloves and safety glasses when cutting copper. Add a variety of beads and a wire-wrapped large marble in colors to complement the copper and black. Purchase a glass votive holder that is flared toward the top or at the rim; this is necessary to make it stay in the holder.

Here's an alternate method to achieve the witch silhouette and bat shapes: use thin craft foam. But if you use this method, DO NOT use the candle and holder, as the shapes could melt. Cut two witch shapes and as many bat shapes as desired. Also cut a witch shape out of thin cardboard, such as a tablet back. Sandwich the cardboard between the foam witch shapes and glue them together. Place it under a book and let it dry. Then treat these shapes as indicated in the instructions.

This project will take approximately 1 hour to complete.

This project's cost will vary according to the kind and number of shapes and beads purchased. The copper sheet, piping and wire will cost about $15.00. Purchase the copper piping and wire at a hardware or home improvement store.

1 Prepare pattern for the moon shape from a thin piece of cardboard such as a manila folder. Mark an 8-inch circle on cardboard. Cut circle. Use curve just cut to mark inside curve of moon. Cut. Trace moon pattern on copper with felt-tipped marker. Tip: Do not place pattern edge close to edge of copper, if possible, as it is harder to cut along an edge with tin snips. Cut moon and cut off the pointed tips to make it safer.

Mark holes to be punched in moon about ¼ inch in from the edges. Mark a hole at each point, centered between edges about ¼ inch in. Mark holes equidistant around

Materials & Tools

- 1 (8 by 10) copper sheet
- 12 inches copper tubing, ¼ inch
- 1 (24-gauge) package copper wire
- 1 (18-gauge) package copper wire
- Metal shapes – 1 witch and 6 to 10 bats
- Beads, miscellaneous – as many as desired
- 1 large marble
- Votive holder with a flared top/rim
- Scrap wood – for using under copper when punching holes
- Steel wool
- Felt-tip marker
- Thin cardboard for pattern
- Thin craft foam, black – one sheet
- Thin piece of cardboard
- Glue
- Tin snips
- Wire cutter
- Long-nosed pliers
- Awl
- Hammer
- Pipe cutter

both sides of the moon, between 1¼ and 1½ inches apart. Add an extra hole at each point, in about ¼ inch. Place moon on scrap board and punch marked holes with awl and hammer.

Use steel wool to polish and remove remaining marks. Punch holes at top of other shapes if they do not have holes.

Cut 12 inches of copper tubing with a pipe cutter. If you do not have a pipe cutter, use tin snips. The tubing will pinch together, but leave it that way. Place a chopstick less than ¼ inch inside tubing. Mark a hole ¼ inch in from end of tubing; turn it over and mark ¼ inch in on the opposite side. Place on scrap board and punch holes. Do the same at the other end of tubing.

2 Thread thin wire through holes in moon starting at point and going over the edges. Secure at each end by making an extra wrap of wire around point, and end wire at back, tucking it under a wire. Using thick wire, cut a length about 26 inches long. Put one end through top extra hole and twist to secure. Determine how long you want this wire in order to make the moon hang properly. Thread remaining end through extra hole at bottom of moon and secure. Twist a loop at the top for hanging.

Holding from the wire, place moon to a surface and determine the lowest point of moon. Mark two horizontal holes, about 1¼ inches up from bottom and ¾ inch apart. Cut a thick wire about 30 inches long and wrap it three to four times around the votive holder leaving about 4 inches of wire at both ends. Put ends through the holes in moon, pull tightly and twist.

3 Insert length of thick wire in top of witch and twist end to secure. Attach to one end of tubing, going through holes. Adjust the length later. Place tubing into wire loop holding the moon. The tubing with witch should hang about 3 inches ahead of moon, far enough not to be affected by the burning candle. Hang the mobile to finish it.

To counterbalance the witch, wrap a large marble with thick wire. Add several bat shapes by wrapping them with a piece of thick wire. Make a hook at the end. Attach the wire to the end of the tubing. Add the marble and it should be balanced. Make any adjustments to make it hang as desired. Indent the tubing gently with wire cutters at the spot where it balances. Wrap thick wire around both sides a few times to hold it in place and create a loop for hanging. Finish any ends of wire by smoothly wrapping it around tubing. Add beads and more bats with the thin wire, as desired.

FALLEN LEAVES TABLE TOPPER

Bring autumn leaves and colors inside to your table for Thanksgiving or almost any other

special occasion.

Make this table topper small or large enough for your dining table. Alter the design as desired from leaves at the corners to a border of leaves or an overall leaf motif. Use a purchased tablecloth or make one. Use the smaller table topper diagonally on an accent table, layered on top of a larger tablecloth.

Make the leaf prints from real leaves that have been dried and pressed or artificial leaves (which are more durable during the printing process). Add detail with sponging and 3-D fabric paints. Use fabric paints and choose the color of the tablecloth in the rich fall range of colors, but make sure your selection is light enough to subtly show the design. Also choose metallic, iridescent or shiny paints for the details of sponging and dimension. As a finishing touch, the beaded fringe adds sparkle and picks up the design's colors. It also adds weight to make the tablecloth hang nicely. Fringe is optional; it makes the tablecloth more formal or elegant. Choose your tablecloth or fabric and fringe first, then choose paints that coordinate.

This project will take approximately 2 hours to complete.

The cost of the paints and artificial leaves is about $12.00. The tablecloth cost can vary greatly; however, the fabric cost can be as low as $6.00 for 2 yards of cotton quilting-weight fabric, which will make a 44-inch-square table topper. Beaded fringe trim varies in price. Step-by-step photos are shown on a lighter-colored fabric to show detail.

Materials & Tools

- Tablecloth or 2 yards of cotton fabric in a quilting weight
- Fabric paints – four or five in fall colors such as burnt orange, red, brown, burgundy and metallic gold
- 3 (3-D) fabric paints in iridescent or shiny brown, copper and red
- 3 (½-inch-wide) paintbrushes — one for each color fabric paint
- Sponge
- Real or artificial leaves
- Thin pieces of cardboard
- Freezer or wax paper
- Paper plate
- Beaded fringe trim (optional) — measure edge of tablecloth

Craft Tips

- Make sure leaves are pressed.
- Wash fabric or purchased tablecloth to remove sizing.
- This project will take some time, practice and concentration … but it's a fun and rewarding process.
- When the project is completed, it can be sprayed with a stain-resistant product. To care for the finished tablecloth, hand wash gently in mild soap and hang to dry. Press from the wrong side to remove wrinkles. If beads are not added, the tablecloth can be washed on the gentle cycle in the machine.
- Practice all the painting techniques on a scrap piece of fabric similar in color and texture.

1 Wash and dry tablecloth or fabric and press. Practice all parts of design on a fabric of similar color and type. Cover work surface with shiny side of freezer paper facing up and tape in place. Apply paint to leaves away from fabric to avoid any spills on fabric, and use freezer paper under that area also. Cut pieces of thin cardboard slightly larger than largest leaf. Determine placement of leaves on fabric, using various sizes and shapes of leaves. (Tip: If the work surface is not large enough to hold entire tablecloth, fold tablecloth in half or quarters if necessary. If the entire project is laid out flat, do all leaves of same size and color at once. If the project needs to be folded, complete all printing in one area and be sure paint is dry before moving to another design area. The 3-D paint will take the longest to dry.)

Start with largest leaf and paint the back side of the leaf, so veins will show. Use enough paint to cover leaf well, but not in globs. To make two-tone leaves, add red paint along the edges of leaf. Place leaf on fabric and cover with piece of cardboard. Holding cardboard securely in place, rub hand over cardboard applying pressure. Lift cardboard and then leaf. Leaves can also be overlapped. If reusing leaves, rinse them before too much paint builds up and press between paper towels to dry.

2 Pour metallic paint on to paper plate. Dab sponge into paint and blot on plate. Apply sponging around leaves, as desired. Sponge can continue to other areas of tablecloth such as the border or center of tablecloth. Let dry.

3 Using 3-D fabric paint, apply from bottle to areas of leaves to highlight design. Long smooth lines are not necessary. Do portions of the edge or veins for an artistic appearance. Let dry. The entire project should dry flat according to manufacturer's directions, usually 24 to 48 hours. Then apply bead fringe trim by machine, with fabric glue or fusible webbing, if desired.

ETCHED GLASS CANDLE HOLDER AND DECORATIVE CANDLE

Create a personalized piece of etched glass easily at home. You will love coming up with new possibilities for etching.

Etching is a long-cherished glass craft. Learning how to do it at home is a great way to embellish many different glass containers. Friends and family will be sure to enjoy the permanence of an etched gift. For a variation, etch a design onto glass jars or a vase. The possibilities are endless. Personalize items with names or special dates to remember. Use a die cutter or craft punches to create many different designs easily.

This project will take approximately 1 hour to complete and cost about $40.00.

1 Use contact paper or a sticky sheet of paper to cut out shapes to apply to the glass container. Choose shapes with a fall theme. (As a variation, choose any kind of decorative shapes desired. Visit your local specialty paper store to use a die cutter, or you can use a craft punch instead. Utilizing these tools is an easy way to save time on drawing and cutting out each shape.) If desired, create your own unique shapes. Just draw right on contact paper. For this example, use a die cutter to punch out two oak leaves to apply to the container.

Next, wash and dry the glass container. Peel off the paper backing on the leaves and arrange them on the glass. For a slight variation on this piece, punch out several more leaves and place them all over the container. When sticking the shapes on the glass, make sure there are no air bubbles and there is a tight seal along the edges.

2 Place the glass container in a plastic pitcher. Only use this pitcher for etching. Do not use the pitcher again for consumables. Fill the glass container with some rocks to weight it down when it is soaking in liquid. Fill the pitcher with water to the top of the glass container. Pull the glass container out and place a water level mark on the pitcher. Read and follow instructions on the back of the bottle of etch bath. In a well-ventilated area, wear gloves and carefully stir the etch bath. Pour the etch bath in the pitcher up to the water level mark. Carefully place the glass container into the etch bath. Let it soak for 5 to 10 minutes, depending on the hardness of the glass. Remove the glass container and wash it under running water. Peel off the sticky paper. Pour the etch bath back into its bottle for reuse. Wash the pitcher and rubber gloves to use again for etching.

3 Decorate the candle with diamond dust glitter. This type of glitter is made from finely ground glass, giving the decorated object a sugared look. Cut some length off the bottom of the candle if it is too tall. Use a paintbrush and decoupage medium to create designs on the candle. Make swirls and dots or any type of design desired. Over a paper plate, shake diamond dust glitter over each design. Pour the excess glitter back into its container. Then pour sand at the bottom of the candle holder to help keep the melted wax from sticking to the bottom of the glass. Place the decorated candle inside the etched glass candle holder and enjoy. Do not leave candle burning while it is unattended.

Craft Tip
• Visit your local specialty paper store to use a die cutter, or you can use a craft punch.

FALL CHAIR DRESSING

Every guest at your table will feel extra-special by sitting in a "dressed" and decorated chair this fall.

For the finishing touch to your autumn table, dress the chairs with beautiful fabric, ribbon, raffia and a fall bouquet! Here are instructions for making a muslin pattern to make your own chair dressings. Then choose a solid-colored fabric that complements your decor.

This project will take approximately 1 hour to make the pattern, 30 to 45 minutes per chair to cut out fabric and sew, and 15 minutes to assemble and tie the bouquet on the chair.

The pattern for this project will cost about $6.00. For each finished chair, fabric will be the price per yard times three (yards). The bouquet will cost about $12.00.

1 Make a pattern for the chair dressing. Drape inexpensive muslin over the chair, starting at the bottom back of the chair and draping over the top of the chair and over the seat of the chair, allowing an inch or more for a hem in the back. Weight the fabric down on the seat of the chair by using unopened food cans. Pin the fabric together, creating side seams, at the sides of the chair, down to the seat. If the chair is rounded at the top (like the chair shown), pin the fabric down at the curves of the chair near the top. Cut away all excess fabric, leaving ½-inch extra fabric for seams.

Materials & Tools

- 3 yards of inexpensive 44- to 45-inch muslin (for pattern)
- 3 yards of 4-inch ribbon per chair
- Raffia (long strands)
- Artificial sunflowers
- Artificial berries
- Twigs
- Sewing machine
- Straight pins
- Scissors

Craft Tip

- To change the look for a different season or holiday, simply remove the ribbon and bouquet, and add a new ribbon and bouquet, ornaments or even photocopies of family members to dress the chairs for all your special occasions.

2 This piece will be a rectangle. Measure the distance between the two side seams of the chair covering, going around the front of the chair, and the distance from the top of the chair seat to the floor. Be sure to add ½ inch at each side and the top for the seam allowances and an inch or more at the bottom for the hem. Cut out the muslin and pin it to the side seams and around the front of the chair.

3 Assemble a bouquet from the sunflowers, berries and twigs, tying it together with a piece of raffia. Wrap the ribbon around the chair, and tie on the bouquet at the back of the chair. Tie long strands of raffia around the ribbon and bouquet, and tie a bow. Or you can knot the raffia and make an additional decorative bow to add to the front of the bouquet. If necessary, use safety pins from the back to anchor the bouquet at the top.

4 Fabrics come in various widths, so take your two muslin pattern pieces with you to the fabric store, and lay them out on your desired fabric to determine how much yardage you will need to cover as many chairs as you want.

Lay the muslin pattern pieces on the fabric and cut them out. To begin, drape the back/top/chair piece with the RIGHT SIDE DOWN. When pinning the skirt piece onto the chair top, pin the fabric RIGHT SIDES TOGETHER. Follow the instructions above to assemble the chair dressing, pinning and sewing the chair side seams, and then pinning and sewing the skirt onto the chair top. Turn and pin the bottom of the fabric up to sew the hem.

FALL
GARDENING

Fall is a great time to be in the garden. It's also a great time to be a plant. Cool nights, warm days, and a good dash of rainfall here and there, make for perfect growing conditions for flowers. That's why you've got to do a little planning ahead, then get out there now and assure that those autumn blooms come through. Vegetables thrive in autumn too ... so don't give up on fresh produce just because frosty nights are coming, or already here.

Facing page: Wildflower Gardens, page 123

Autumn Knot Garden

Create a colorful autumn accent using hardy chrysanthemums.

As the perennials in your garden begin to show the effects of a long, hot summer, consider adding fresh color with a miniature knot garden—created from hardy mums for a quick fall display. Knot gardens use symmetrically designed geometric patterns to achieve the illusion of interlaced plants. They became fashionable in Europe during the 16th and 17th centuries and are popular today as a distinct accent for small areas.

Materials & Tools

- Brick or stone pavers for border
- Graph paper
- Tape measure, string, stakes and level
- Trowel and rake
- Circular or semicircular stepping-stones
- Low-growing hardy mum plants
  (We used 30 4½-inch pots.)
- Mulch or gravel

Garden Tips

- Knot gardens are best suited for flat areas. Consider a seldom-used space, such as the narrow strip between your garage and the neighbor's, if it's sunny enough.
- Keep the line of the garden neat and shapes of plants clipped.
- Water in the morning so foliage can dry before nightfall. Plants packed tightly together are susceptible to fungal diseases.
- Consider adding a birdbath or sculpture to the center of your knot garden.

How To Create Your Knot Garden

1 Choose a square or rectangular area that is flat and able to be seen from above, as from a deck or a window. Once you have chosen your site, lay out the dimensions on graph paper. Our space measured approximately 6 feet by 3 feet. Keeping in mind the size of your garden, create your own simple geometric design—or search the library or Internet for knot garden designs.

2 Define the space by making a border for your garden. We used brick pavers laid end to end, but you also could outline the space with timbers or plants, such as clipped boxwood. Make sure the soil is level, and adjust the bricks as you go. Check your dimensions to keep it square—a level comes in handy here.

3 Transfer your patterned layout to the garden using a tape measure, string and stake to create circles and semicircles. Consider adding stepping-stones in the circular areas of your garden. Many styles are available at your garden center.

4 Choose hardy mum plants that are short and well-flowered so your design fills in quickly. Planting the mums closely together will ensure the design is complete on the day you plant it.

5 Finish off your garden with a complementary mulch or gravel. Small round materials, such as bark chips, pea gravel, or cocoa bean shells, fill in around the plants and accent the shapes nicely.

6 Water your garden thoroughly. Don't be afraid to pinch and prune your plants regularly to create the continuous ribbon effect that is unique to knot gardens.

LATE-SEASON STUNNERS

Grow perennials that add color and interest in autumn.

Looking for a splash of late-fall color? If your garden fades long before the snow flies, it's time to add some plants that don't stop shining when the weather turns cold.

Early autumn is a good time to both evaluate new plants and, in many cases, to add new perennials to your garden. The perennials will start putting down roots in the warm soil, and come spring, they'll get a jump start on the season.

Autumn is also a good time to take a stroll to your local home garden centers. Some have bargain prices on perennials left from the season; others may have test plots where they evaluate new releases before adding them to their sales collection for next year.

Also take a walk through your community and take note of what is shining in your neighbors' gardens right now. Knock on the door if you see something intriguing and ask what it is. Nothing pleases gardeners more than showing off their treasures.

When you find a plant you like, pay particular attention to the exact name. Some plant families have species that bloom at different times of the year or that grow in different forms (tall, short, trailing and so on). Anemones, for example, have both spring- and autumn-flowering varieties; the spring ones are short, the fall ones are tall.

In addition, some garden centers stock potted perennials all summer and fall is an excellent time to add these plants to your garden. Mulch late-planted specimens heavily to prevent the frost from heaving them out of the ground.

Here are a few favorite fall performers to consider.

Anemone

While many gardeners are familiar with anemones as spring- and summer-bloomers, Chinese and Japanese anemones (*Anemone hupehensis* and *A. x hybrida*) bloom into autumn. These types have divided leaves and flower in charming shades of white and pink. These plants thrive in partial to full sun in moist but well-drained soil that's rich in organic matter. Both types are generally hardy in Zones 4 to 8, but may need extra protection in the northern portions of this range. The tallest types can grow to 5 feet.

Be on the watch for 'September Charm', which offers pink flowers; 'Prince Henry', with its rose-pink blooms, and 'Whirlwind', which has semi-double white flowers.

Anemones can spread rapidly in ideal conditions, and they can be propagated by division in autumn.

Aster

Asters (*Aster* spp.) are one of the old standards when it comes to autumn-blooming perennials. Asters bloom in a wide range of colors—white, pink, red, mauve, purple, blue and even yellow. New England asters (*Aster novae-angliae*) and Michaelmas daisies (*A. novi-belgii*), are both natives of North America, and are among the most common. They can reach 5 feet and bear purple flowers. 'Purple Dome', a dwarf-type resistant to powdery mildew, is one of the best. *A. lateriflorus* 'Prince' sports attractive purplish foliage all season and then adds white flowers in fall.

Plant asters in a spot with full sun and good air flow to help

Anemone hupehensis.

Aster 'Purple Dome'.

Pink boltonia and asters.

Sweet autumn clematis.

Geranium endressii *in autumn.*
Inset: *Many geraniums color in fall.*

prevent problems with powdery mildew—a common aster disease that can disfigure the plants by the time they reach their peak bloom.

Boltonia

Boltonia (*Boltonia asteroides*), looks something like a large aster when in bloom: Hardy in Zones 4 to 8, it has many clusters of daisy-like flowers that are white, lilac or purple. A native to areas of North America, it thrives in sunny, well-drained sites.

Two of the most popular cultivars are 'Snowbank', a white-flowering type which is often nearly covered in blossoms, and 'Pink Beauty', a pink-flowering form.

Bugbane brings color to the back of the border.

Both grow to 5 feet or more. Some gardeners consider boltonia weedy when it's not in bloom; be sure to judge for youself!

Bugbane

Bugbane (*Cimicifuga* spp.), sometimes called snakeroot or black cohosh, is a tall, autumn-flowering perennial with attractive divided leaves. Bugbanes bloom with airy "wands" of white flowers that may carry an unpleasant odor. (Plant them where you can see but not smell them!) Some bugbanes, such as *C. racemosa* (a North American native), stretch as high as 7 feet, making them a back-of-the-border plant. Others (*C. simplex*, for instance) top out around 4 feet. Some newer cultivars, such as 'Brunette', offer burgundy foliage.

Bugbanes prefer moist but well-drained spots in partial shade. Hardiness varies by species; the hardiest grow in Zones 3 to 8.

Sweet Autumn Clematis

You may be drawn to this beautiful vine by its fragrance. Unlike most other clematis, the sweet autumn clematis (*Clematis terniflora*, sometimes referred to as *C. paniculata* or *C. maximowicziana*) puts on its flower show in fall, as its name suggests.

Numerous small, white, fragrant flowers give way to fluffy, silvery seed heads. This vine can eventually grow to 20 feet and is hardy in Zones 4 to 9. Like other clematis, it prefers to have its roots shaded in moist, but well-drained soil and its foliage exposed to all-day sun.

Geranium

While not true fall bloomers (their season lasts most of the summer), many perennial geraniums (*Geranium sanguineum*, *G. erianthum* and *G. eriostemon*, for instance) add spice to the fall garden with beautifully colored foliage. A few species, such as pink-flowering *Geranium endressii*, bloom into autumn and are valuable for adding even more color. Hardiness varies by species; many grow in Zones 4 to 7.

Plant geraniums in a sunny to partial shade spot with moist but well-drained soil that's high in organic matter for best results.

Globe Thistle

Globe thistle (*Echinops* spp.), is a favorite of many dried-flower arrangers. While not a true fall bloomer (it starts its show as early as midsummer), this is a long-lasting plant that holds interest into fall with spiny, thistle-like foliage and

Globe thistle.

Goldenrod, an autumn favorite.

A perennial sunflower—Helianthus angustifolius.

gray-blue, globe-shaped flowers. Ultimate plant height and hardiness vary by species—most grow from 2 to 5 feet tall and are hardy Zones 3 to 8.

A couple of outstanding cultivars to watch for are 'Veitch's Blue'—a re-bloomer with darker gray-blue flowerheads than most—and 'Taplow Blue', with larger, brighter blue flowerheads.

In some gardens, globe thistles have a tendency to self-seed, but rarely to the point of being a nuisance. Globe thistle can also be divided in autumn.

Goldenrod

Goldenrod (*Solidago* spp.), another North American native, is easily recognized as a wildflower. Vigorous, hardy plants may grow to 5 feet.

Cultivars such as 'Loddon Gold' have been bred to have showier flowers than the typical wild form, but they are less hardy. The native form, *S. canadensis*, is hardy to Zone 3 and bears fluffy flowers in shades of gold at the end of summer and through autumn. As is the case with many natives, goldenrod may spread quickly in garden

conditions—full sun and fertile, well-drained soil.

Helenium

Helenium spp., a North American native known as sneezeweed, has a number of excellent long-flowering cultivars that bear daisy-like flowers in shades of yellow to red to rusty-brown. The plants grow best in spots with full sun and moist but well-drained soil. Some cultivars to watch for include 'Bressingham Gold', with gold flowers, and copper-colored 'Crimson Beauty'. They are hardy Zones 4 to 8.

Sneezeweed.

Helianthus

While many gardeners may be more familiar with sunflowers (*Helianthus* spp.) as annuals, there are some that bloom in autumn. One of the most common is *H. maximilliani*, which bears many smaller, bright yellow flowers. This North American native can grow to more than 9 feet in ideal conditions and is hardy Zones 4 to 9. A cultivar to watch for is 'Capenoch Star'.

One note: Some species of perennial sunflower spread rapidly in moist soil and become a pest in the garden. Plant this where its more exuberant tendencies won't matter.

Joe Pye Weed

Butterflies and bees seem to love the fluffy pink flowers topping Joe Pye weed (*Eupatorium purpureum*). This native plant is easy to grow in a moist, sunny site in Zones 3 to 9.

Joe Pye weed can grow to more than 6 feet in an ideal site, but usually stays around 4 to 5 feet. One cultivar to watch for is 'Chocolate'—a purple-leafed, white-flowering form of *E. rugosum*, a closely related species. Joe

Tall Joe Pye weed.

Mass rudbeckias for impact.

Sedum 'Autumn Joy'.

Pye weed can also be propagated by division in fall.

Lilyturf

Lilyturf (*Liriope muscari*) looks like an ornamental grass until it sends up spikes of purplish or white flowers in fall. These sometimes aggressive ground covers grow to about a foot and are hardy in Zones 6 to 10.

Lilyturfs are drought-tolerant and prefer a shady spot in the garden. Be on the lookout for cultivars such as 'Silver Dragon', which has silver-variegated foliage, and 'Lilac Beauty', which has lilac-colored flower spikes.

Rudbeckia

Coneflowers, or black-eyed Susans (*Rudbeckia* spp.), bear yellow or orangish flowers in late summer and autumn. Most species are native to areas of North America and are well-adapted to garden life. A number of species are great garden plants—*R. fulgida* and *R. hirta* are the most common. Both species grow to about 3 feet. Many species are hardy as far north as Zone 3.

Some species of coneflower self-seed readily in the garden and can become something of a pest.

Sedum

One of the sure-bets for an autumn garden, *Sedum* 'Autumn Joy' bears dense clusters of pink flowers that eventually fade to a warm bronze. Related 'Brilliant' is known for its bright pink flowers; 'Frosty Morn' is a favorite for its variegated foliage and is attractive even when not in bloom.

Sedums require well-drained soils and a sunny spot for the best flowering and can, in ideal conditions, reach nearly 2 feet. Hardy in Zones 4 to 9.

Toad Lilies

Toad lilies (*Tricyrtis* spp.) are another must-have autumn-bloomer for shady spots in the garden. Small, orchid-like flowers in shades of white, pink, purple and sometimes even yellow top these delicate plants. The hardiest species, *T. hirta*, grows in Zones 4 to 9 and needs a moist but well-drained soil that's high in organic matter. *T.* 'White Towers' is known for its white flowers; 'White Flame' is grown for its variegated foliage and purple-spotted white flowers. Most toad lilies grow to about 3 feet.

Grassy lilyturf.

Plant toad lilies in shade.

AUTUMN'S EVERLASTING ANNUALS

This fall, preserve your garden's color and beauty with the traditional but seasonal techniques of pressing and drying flowers.

One of the easiest ways to surround yourself with beautiful flowers year-round is to include everlasting annuals in your garden. These are flowers that retain their forms and colors after they are dried. Everlastings can do this because their showy petals are not really petals at all. Instead, they are papery bracts or, in some cases, calyxes, which contain much less moisture than true petals. After they are cut and brought indoors to dry in a warm, dark place, many everlasting flowers keep their good looks for years.

In the garden, everlastings are every bit as beautiful as other flowers, so it's fine to feature them in mixed flower beds or a cutting garden. All everlastings are sun lovers, and you will harvest the most blooms if you grow them in fertile soil that has been amended with organic matter. It's a happy coincidence that everlasting annuals often can get by on less water than other annuals. In fact, dry conditions near harvest time often enhance the staying power of the blossoms.

In addition to collecting and drying delicate blossoms, don't overlook decorative seedpods, such as those produced by nigella and poppy, or feathery plumes of amaranth or celosia. They will come in handy on the gray winter day when you decide to create a refreshing wreath or arrangement from flowers and seeds gathered months before.

Pretty Pressed Flowers

Numerous small flowers such as pansies and brachychome can be dried via the process called pressing. You can use a flower press, or simply arrange leaves and blossoms between sheets of waxed paper and place them between the pages of a heavy telephone directory for several weeks. When they are completely dried, gently glue them onto greeting cards, arrange them on a piece of mat board and frame them, or use them to decorate homemade candles or decoupage items.

If you have access to a color copy machine, you might enjoy making collages of leaves and small blossoms by a more modern method. Arrange any flat flowers and leaves on the glass bed of the machine, and press go. Photocopied flowers don't have the antique look of those that are

Strawflowers including acroclinium *(left) and* helichrysum *(right) are among the most beloved of all dried flowers. Protected from extreme humidity, they will keep their good looks indefinitely.*

pressed to dry, but it's a fast and fun project that fascinates children of all ages.

Pansies, ammi and numerous other flowers are simple to dry in a flower press or heavy phone book. After drying, glue the blossoms onto note cards for a lovely personal touch, or imbed them in homemade candles.

Drying Everlastings, Step-by-Step

1 Most everlasting flowers are best picked when the blossoms are about halfway open. With flowers that form spikes and open gradually from the bottom to the top (such as bells of Ireland and blue salvia), wait until at least two-thirds of the flowers are open. Choose perfect blossoms that have not been damaged by wind, water or insects.

2 Harvest when the flowers are completely dry. Late morning, after the dew has dried, is the best time. Cut all flowers with long stems attached, even if you must remove a few buds along with the blossoms (buds often dry well too). Gather more material than you think you will need. Blossoms shrink a little as they dry, and the best dried flower crafts and arrangements are packed with plenty of blossoms.

3 Strip off all of the leaves from each stem; they slow the drying process and can host molds and mildews. Sort your flowers into small bunches of 10 to 12 stems, and secure the ends with rubber bands. Very large stems that tend to bend, such as amaranth and bells of Ireland, are best dried singly. Hang the stems or bunches upside down from nails or pegs (a bent paper clip inserted into the rubber band makes a great hanging hook). To save space, use clothespins to clip three small bunches to a wire clothes hanger.

4 Hang the prepared stems in a warm, well-ventilated place that does not receive strong sunlight. A garage, storage room, or closet is better than a stuffy attic, where conditions may be too hot. Use a small fan if necessary to keep the air circulating freely. Under good conditions, your flowers should be thoroughly dry in 1 to 2 weeks.

5 Store your dried flowers in airtight boxes. To simplify storage, you can use brown florist tape to bind together small bunches of slender flowers such as gomphrena. When you make a wreath or arrangement, use the bundle the same way you'd use a single stem in an arrangement of fresh flowers.

Make Your Own Potpourri

Collect dried blossoms that break or shatter and put them aside in a large jar to use as base for homemade potpourri. Also collect and dry blossoms and petals from other flowers removed during routine deadheading, including calendula, cosmos, marigold, verbena and roses. Transform your collected dried material into potpourri by scenting small batches with essential oils of your choice. After adding the oils, let the mixture infuse in a closed jar for at least a week.

Bells of Ireland are easy to grow and fun to dry. Expect the stems and bracts to become slightly distorted as they dry. You can trim away unsightly parts when you're ready to use the dried stems.

To make your dried flowers smell as good as they look, infuse your homegrown potpourri mixture with a few drops of essential oil. Avoid synthetic scents if you are prone to allergies.

AUTUMN GLORY: WILDFLOWER GARDENS

Fall is the time to start a spectacular wildflower garden.

Whether it's a huge swath of wildflowers serving as a beautiful buffer between the house and the forest (above) or a small patch of native beauties right outside the door (inset), wildflowers are amazingly adaptable plants.

When most people think of wildflowers, they see them as suitable only for large plantings—plantings measured in acres instead of square feet. Nothing could be further from the truth. Wildflowers are a great, low-maintenance addition to yards of any size, whether the wildflowers are planted in traditional bor-

ders, in that rough area "out back" or as a replacement for a grass lawn.

Wildflower experts agree that the time when wild flowers are in their glory—in spring and summer—really isn't the best time to plant them. While it's certainly possible to have a successful wildflower garden

Wildflowers (as seen here and bottom right) have a natural charm that's hard to resist. Somewhat surprisingly, most make excellent, long-lasting cut flowers.

Garden Tip
Care of the Wildflower Meadow

In every climate, there are rampant weeds unworthy of the wildflower meadow. Here's how to tame them:

- Hoe, pull out or chop down large aggressive weeds before they shed seeds.

- Mark the locations of tough perennial weeds with a stake and dig them out during the winter.

- Mow down wildflowers any time there is not a major species on the brink of bloom:

  - In most areas, late fall is the best time to mow.

  - Allow time for your favorite species to shower the ground with seeds before you mow.

  - Leave the "wildflower hay" on the ground. It is probably chock full of good seeds.

Basic care leads to wildflowers galore!

by planting the seeds in spring, you simply increase your chances for success by planting in the fall.

By planting in the fall, home gardeners take advantage of a cycle that naturally takes place in the wild. Native wildflowers bloom and set seed in the spring and autumn. The seed falls to ground or is spread from one location to another by birds and other animals. As the days grow shorter, temperatures drop and winter's rain or snow arrives. The seed lies dormant through the winter, snug in the soil, just waiting to sprout during the first longer, warmer days of spring.

There's something unique about the beauty of wildflowers, unmatched by more "cultivated" flowers. Wildflowers have a natural, casual beauty that goes straight to the heart of gardening, and they fit easily into suburban surroundings. And as a bonus, free-flowering wildflowers make great cut flowers for surprisingly long-lasting bouquets.

Unfortunately, a fair amount of misinformation regarding wildflowers has made its way into print. For the greatest success with wildflowers, heed the following advice:

- Make sure the wildflower mix you buy is either specially formulated for your geographic region or for specific conditions, such as dry or shady locations.

- Be a comparison shopper. Find out what wildflower varieties are in a mix and how many ounces of actual wildflower seed is contained in the package—and then compare costs. Some packagers bulk up their mixes with a disproportionate amount of clover or other common seed.

- In the high-rainfall areas of the Midwest, a seed mix should contain a high proportion of perennial wildflowers. With warm spring and summer temperatures and high rainfall, plant growth is rapid in these regions and perennial species tend to naturally dominate the landscape. If you live in the Far West or Southwest, the arid summer conditions there require different mixes, with an emphasis on annual varieties—ones which reseed readily from one year to the next.

- If at all possible, plant wildflower seeds in the fall. Although they can be planted in the early spring, fall-planted wildflowers perform much better because the gardener is working in harmony with the natural rhythm of nature.

- Take the time to properly prepare the soil before planting the seed. This idea, combined with purchasing the best quality seed for your area, virtually ensures the success of any wildflower planting.

- There are plenty of fall-blooming wildflowrs to bring color and beauty to your yard during this season. Two favorites are asters and goldenrod.

- Birds love the seeds wildflowers leave on the ground and in their seed heads.

How To
Plant a New Wildflower Meadow

1 In fall, set the cutting blade on your mower as low as possible and scalp off all existing weeds and grasses. Rake up the clippings. If you prefer, treat the area with a glyphosate herbicide three weeks before planting your wildflower seeds.

2 Cultivate the surface of the soil, but go only 1 inch deep. Deep cultivation often increases weed problems. Rake over the surface.

3 Broadcast seeds of hardy species over the surface, distributing them in an even pattern. Walk over the area to press the seeds into the loose soil.

4 In dry or windy climates, barely cover the seeded soil with a light sprinkling of weed-free wheat or oat straw so that you can see the soil's surface between pieces of straw.

5 In early spring, rake open spaces where wildflower seedlings are evident, and sow them with annuals species as described in Step 3.

Try These
Best Wildflowers by Region

*Mexican hat (*Ratibida columnaris*) is just one of the many wildflowers content to grow over most parts of the country.*

Wildflowers for the Northeast
Baby's breath (*Gypsophila muralis*)
Black-eyed Susan (*Rudbeckia hirta*)
Blanket flower (*Gaillardia aristata*)
Blue flax (*Linum lewisii*)
Catchfly (*Silene armeria*)
Cornflower (*Centaurea cyanus*)
Corn poppy (*Papaver rhoeas*)
Dame's rocket (*Hesperis matronalis*)
Evening primrose (*Oenothera lamarchiana*)
Foxglove (*Digitalis pupurea*)
Indian blanket (*Gaillardia pulchella*)
Northeast aster (*Aster novae-angliae*)
Perennial lupine (*Lupinus perennis*)
Plains coreopsis/calliopsis (*Coreopsis tinctoria*)
Purple coneflower (*Echinacea purpurea*)
Rocket larkspur (*Delphinium ajacus*)
Scarlet flax (*Linum rubrum*)
Shasta daisy (*Chrysanthemum maximum*)
Tickseed (*Coreopsis lanceolata*)
Wallflower (*Cheiranthus allionii*)
Yarrow (*Achillea millefolium*)

Wildflowers for the North Central States
Baby's breath (*Gypsophila muralis*)
Black-eyed Susan (*Rudbeckia hirta*)
Blanket flower (*Gaillardia aristata*)
Catchfly (*Silene armeria*)
Clasping coneflower (*Rudbeckia amplexicaulis*)
Cornflower (*Centaurea cyanus*)
Corn poppy (*Papaver rhoeas*)
Dame's rocket (*Hesperis matronalis*)
Evening primrose (*Oenothera lamarchiana*)
Indian blanket (*Gaillardia pulchella*)
Lemon mint (*Monarda citriodora*)
Mexican hat (*Ratibida columnaris*)
Missouri primrose (*Oenothera missouriensis*)
Perennial lupine (*Lupinus perennis*)
Plains coreopsis (*Coreopsis tinctoria*)
Purple coneflower (*Echinacea purpurea*)
Purple prairie clover (*Petalostemum purpureum*)
Rocket larkspur (*Delphinium ajacis*)
Scarlet flax (*Linum rubrum*)
Tahoka daisy (*Machaeranthera tanacetifolia*)
Tickseed (*Coreopsis lanceolata*)
Toadflax (*Linaria maroccana*)
Yarrow (*Achillea millefolium*)

Wildflowers for the Southeast
African daisy (*Dimorphotheca aurantica*)
Black-eyed Susan (*Rudbeckia hirta*)
Clasping coneflower (*Rudbeckia amplexicaulis*)
Cornflower (*Centaurea cyanus*)
Corn poppy (*Papaver rhoeas*)
Cosmos (*Cosmos bipinnatus*)
Dame's rocket (*Hesperis matronalis*)
Drummond phlox (*Phlox drummondii*)
Dwarf red plains coreopsis (*Coreopsis tinctoria*)
Evening primrose (*Oenothera lamarchiana*)
Five spot (*Nemophila maculata*)

Indian blanket (*Gaillardia pulchella*)
Lemon mint (*Monarda citriodora*)
Mexican hat (*Ratibida columnaris*)
Moss verbena (*Verbena tenuisecta*)
Plains coreopsis (*Coreopsis tinctoria*)
Purple coneflower (*Echinacea purpurea*)
Rocket larkspur (*Delphinium ajacis*)
Scarlet flax (*Linum rubrum*)
Showy primrose (*Oenothera speciosa*)
Sweet alyssum (*Lobularia maritima*)
Tickseed (*Coreopsis lanceolata*)
Toadflax (*Linaria maroccana*)
Yarrow (*Achillea millefolium*)

Wildflowers for the Rocky Mountain States
Black-eyed Susan (*Rudbeckia hirta*)
Blanket flower (*Gaillardia aristata*)
Blue flax (*Linum lewisii*)
Catchfly (*Silene armeria*)
Clasping coneflower (*Rudbeckia amplexicaulis*)
Cornflower (*Centaurea cyanus*)
Corn poppy (*Papaver rhoeas*)
Dame's rocket (*Hesperis matronalis*)
Evening primrose (*Oenothera lamarchiana*)
Indian blanket (*Gaillardia pulchella*)
Mexican hat (*Ratibida columnaris*)
Perennial lupine (*Lupinus perennis*)
Rocket larkspur (*Delphinium ajacis*)
Rocky Mountain penstemon (*Penstemon strictus*)
Scarlet flax (*Linum rubrum*)
Shasta daisy (*Chrysanthemum maximum*)
Tahoka daisy (*Machaeranthera tanacetifolia*)
Tickseed (*Coreopsis lanceolata*)
Toadflax (*Linaria maroccana*)
Wallflower (*Cheiranthus allionii*)
Yarrow (*Achillea millefolium*)

Wildflowers for the West
African daisy (*Dimorphotheca aurantica*)
Arroyo lupine (*Lupinus succulentus*)
Baby blue eyes (*Nemophila insignis*)
Birds eyes (*Gilia tricolor*)

Black-eyed Susan (*Rudbeckia hirta*)
Blue flax (*Linum lewisii*)
Catchfly (*Silene armeria*)
California bluebell (*Phacelia campanularia*)
California poppy (*Eschscholzia californica*)
Cornflower (*Centaurea cyanus*)
Dame's rocket (*Hesperis matronalis*)
Five spot (*Nemophila maculata*)
Evening primrose (*Oenothera lamarchiana*)
Indian blanket (*Gaillardia pulchella*)
Plains coreopsis (*Coreopsis tinctoria*)
Perennial lupine (*Lupinus perennis*)
Rocket larkspur (*Delphinium ajacis*)
Rocky Mountain penstemon (*Penstemon strictus*)
Scarlet flax (*Linum rubrum*)
Shasta daisy (*Chrysanthemum maximum*)
Tickseed (*Coreopsis lanceolata*)
Tidytips (*Layia platyglossa*)
Toadflax (*Linaria maroccana*)
Wallflower (*Cheiranthus allionii*)
Yarrow (*Achillea millefolium*)

Wildflowers for the Southwest
African daisy (*Dimorphotheca aurantica*)
Arroyo lupine (*Lupinus succulentus*)
Baby blue eyes (*Nemophila insignis*)
Black-eyed Susan (*Rudbeckia hirta*)
California bluebell (*Phacelia campanularia*)
California poppy (*Eschscholzia californica*)
Clasping coneflower (*Rudbeckia amplexicaulis*)
Five spot (*Nemophila maculata*)
Indian blanket (*Gaillardia pulchella*)
Mexican hat (*Ratibida columnaris*)
Moss verbena (*Verbena tenuisecta*)
Plains coreopsis (*Coreopsis tinctoria*)
Purple tansy (*Phacelia tanacetifolia*)
Scarlet flax (*Linum rubrum*)
Showy primrose (*Oenothera speciosa*)
Tahoka daisy (*Machaeranthera tanacetifolia*)
Tidytips (*Layia platyglossa*)
Toadflax (*Linaria maroccana*)
Yarrow (*Achillea millefolium*)

SIX WAYS TO EXTEND YOUR VEGGIE-GROWING SEASON

With these simple strategies, short-season gardeners can grow fresh vegetables from early spring to late autumn.

In many parts of the country, it seems the growing season is too short to enjoy your favorite vegetables. Luckily, a few simple season-extending techniques will allow you to start savoring your veggies all fall and harvesting them well past your area's autumn frost dates.

There are two ways to lengthen the growing season for edibles: raise the soil temperature to provide an artificially warmer environment for seedlings in spring and provide frost protection for mature plants in fall. These six tips will help you do both.

1. Make or buy a cold frame.

Cold frames are basically miniature, unheated greenhouses made of a wooden frame covered with clear plastic or glass. (You can even use an old storm window.) The enclosure soaks up the sun's warmth during the day and retains that heat at night, raising the air and soil temperature and protecting the plants from below-freezing conditions. You can use cold frames to start cool-weather crops earlier than normal in spring, or you can "harden off" seedlings you've started indoors, giving them a transition period between your house and the garden. In the fall, cold frames allow you to sow cool-weather crops that may linger into early winter if you give them enough moisture and nutrients. Cold frames also shield

plants from wind, hail, insects, and diseases. On sunny days above 45°F, vent the cold frame by propping open or removing the cover, as excessive heat stresses young plants.

2. Build raised beds.

By elevating the soil surface above ground level, you warm the earth faster and help it drain better. Deeper topsoil levels also increase yields. You can use wooden timbers, stones, or cement blocks to build raised beds, though you can achieve a similar effect simply by mounding the soil.

3. Use floating row covers.

Floating row covers are made of a lightweight polypropylene fabric that gently rests on top of your

plants. As the plants grow, they push up the material. The thickest row covers protect down to 25°F. Tiny pores in the translucent fabric allow air and water to get through and permit 70 to 80 percent light transmission. The cloth is kept in place with staples, rocks, soil, or wire hoops. In cold climates, row covers can extend the season by two months or more. When plants begin to flower in the spring, remove the covers so insects can pollinate the flowers. In the fall, use thicker fabric to retain soil heat and protect plants against early frost—you'll be able to harvest heat-loving crops like peppers and tomatoes a few weeks later than normal.

4. Use plastic mulch.

In recent years, more and more gardeners have begun using plastic mulches. They warm the soil, provide higher yields, block out weeds and conserve water and fertilizer. Heat-loving plants such as melons, squash, pumpkins, cucumbers and eggplants grow faster and produce earlier.

The most commonly used mulch is black plastic, which suppresses weeds and raises the surface soil temperature 3 to 5 degrees Fahrenheit. Clear plastic allows greater warming (12 to 15 degrees) and is used most often in northern climates. The biggest disadvantage to clear plastic is that it lets light through, which promotes weed growth.

Scientists have recently developed other colored plastics with unique properties. Infrared-transmitting (IRT) mulch, for example, warms the soil like clear plastic while providing the weed-suppressing properties of black mulch. Using IRT mulch results in earlier harvest dates and larger yields of melons, cucumbers and other crops. IRT plastic comes in brown or blue-green. Red plastic works like black mulch to heat the soil, control weeds and conserve moisture, and United States Department of Agriculture (USDA) research has shown that it increases tomato production by up to 20 percent. Strawberry crops may also benefit. Silver plastic repels some aphid species.

5. Put up barriers around plants.

To protect individual plants, even rudimentary barriers will reduce wind and raise the temperature slightly. Place tomato cages encircled with bubble wrap or plastic jugs with the bottoms removed over the plants. Gallon milk jugs filled with water and placed around plants also have a protective effect.

6. Pick cold-tolerant plant varieties.

If you garden in an area that has a short growing season, it's essential to plant varieties adapted to your climate. Cool-weather plants that perform well in the extreme North include cabbage, kohlrabi, Brussels sprouts and broccoli. For warm-weather plants such as tomatoes and peppers, choose sturdy varieties. Northern gardeners have had success with tomato varieties such as 'Siberia' and 'Polar'.

Some mail-order companies offer seeds bred especially for cold-weather regions. Cold-hardy varieties tolerate chilly temperatures and experience less rot and disease, while short-season varieties grow and mature more quickly than standard types. Some hybrids tolerate autumn's low light conditions and cold temperatures. Before ordering seeds, ask which varieties will do best in your region.

AN EASY AUTUMN TO-DO LIST

Store your harvest, boost your lawn and enjoy the golden months.

Gardeners may view spring as the most important gardening season, but fall has its share of tasks and activities as well. As weather starts to cool, now's the perfect time to ...

- **Plant garlic:** In most regions (except for the very warmest climates), early fall is the best time to plant garlic. Select the healthiest bulblets from nursery or garden-grown bulbs (supermarket bulbs often are treated with growth retardants and may not sprout in your garden). Plant the bulblets 2 inches deep, 6 to 8 weeks before the first frost date in your area. Garlic takes up to 8 months to mature in cold-weather areas and will be ready to harvest next summer.

- **Pamper your lawn:** Fall, rather than spring, is often the best time to fertilize your yard. Grasses can use a boost after the summer's heat. Cool-season grasses (fescues, bluegrass, ryegrass) can build up reserve strength for early green-up next spring. Apply a fertilizer with a nitrogen-phosphorus-potassium (NPK) ratio of 3:1:2 or 4:1:2 (for example, bags marked 6-2-4 or 8-2-4) according to directions.

If you choose to use chemical weedkillers on your lawn, now's also the time to apply those systemic herbicide treatments to attack dandelions, clover and many other weeds. Why? As perennials, these plants store up nutrients in their roots for winter, and treatments applied now will be more effective. Catching these weeds at the proper time minimizes the amount of weedkillers you'll use in the future. (As always, be sure to follow label directions with any herbicide.)

- **Ease back in:** Herbs, geraniums and other tender container-grown plants that have spent the summer outdoors need attention before you bring them back inside. First, inspect them for disease or insects—you don't want to bring infected plants indoors. Wash off your plants with insecticidal soap and the hose to knock off dirt and small insects. Let plants dry off, and then bring them inside for a few hours every day over the course of a week or so. Gradually increase the amount of time plants spend inside until your plants are acclimated to indoor conditions again. If your plant needs cutting back, now is a good time.

With just a little time and effort, you can get your herbs ready for a winter inside.

Garden Tip
Fall Soil Prep Works!

Prepare for spring planting: Remember getting the gardening itch in the spring, only to watch puddles of rain delay your soil prep and dash your hopes for early planting? Well, late fall is a good time to prepare your garden for an early start next season. First, pull out weeds and any plant debris. Dig in or rototill manure, organic matter (shredded leaves, grass, hay) and soil amendments. After a hard frost, cover the beds with a thick layer of mulch or weighted-down plastic. In the spring, just pull back mulch and plant your early cool-weather crops—and let them enjoy all that springtime rain.

Plant Now for Season-Long Bloom

Autumn is the time to plan (and plant) for next spring and summer. Bulbs are the secret!

While bulbous irises aren't as common as those which grow from rhizomes, they're equally elegant. This Dutch iris is 'Purple Sensation', and it's hardy in Zones 5 to 9.

As summer winds down, gardeners start to reflect on the past season. What did well? What didn't? What should I plant next year?

But before you bid this year's garden goodbye, you still have time to add a number of magnificent plants. Granted, they won't bloom until next year, but they'll be worth it when they do.

We're talking, of course, about bulbs. If your garden gets full sun—or at least six hours of it—most of the spring- and summer-blooming bulbs are perfect for you. All of them will offer a show next year that's worth a little work now. You can plant hardy bulbs into the fall as long as the soil stays workable and hasn't frozen.

So, what can I plant this fall, you say? Most alliums, camassias, crocuses, daffodils, snowdrops, hyacinths, lilies and muscari are reliably hardy in Zones 4 to 8 and can be planted this fall in those zones. Fall-planted tulips are happier in the slightly cooler climates of Zones 3 to 7. Less-hardy bulbs, such as *Anemone blanda*, will only bloom reliably next year from a fall planting in Zones 5 to 8. More tender bulbs, such as *Anemone coronaria*, can't be planted in the fall any farther north than Zone 7.

Consult the hardiness rating sidebar on page 134 to find out if fall is a good time for you to plant the favorites listed here. If you live in an area that's too cold for a fall planting, plant these bulbs next spring. If you live in a zone that's too warm for these bulbs, some of which need a period of winter chilling, you can purchase "pre-chilled" bulbs from a number of sources and plant them next year, as well.

That said, it's time to dig in.

Colorful combinations

Part of the fun of building a bulb bed in the fall is anticipating the color combinations that will shine next spring and summer. For instance, while tulips are beautiful by themselves, they can become magi-

Snowflake (Leucojum aestivum) is a delicate white flower hardy in Zones 4 to 9.

The tulip 'Prinses Irene' paired with the annual pansy 'Jolly Joker'.

This daffodil (Narcissus poeticus var. recurvus) is paired with Hyacinthoides 'White Triumphator' (also known as Spanish bluebells). Both plants are hardy in Zones 4 to 10.

cal planted in combination with another color.

Here's an example: A favorite red tulip, 'Temple of Beauty', is one of the tallest single late tulips available. Increase its impact by planting it next to the pristine white bell-shaped flowers of *Leucojum aestivum*. The contrasting colors of this pairing are fantastic!

Another showstopping combination is the fantastic orange and purple tulip 'Prinses Irene'. In spring, surround it with a base planting of the orange and purple pansies 'Jolly Joker'.

Another favorite combo is the tulip 'White Triumphator' combined with the bold blue of *Hyacinthoides hispanica* 'Excelsior'. Or combine a red tulip like the robust, double early 'Abba' or a bright orange tulip like 'Orange Monarch' with the bright blue, easy-growing *Muscari armeniacum*. These are two strong colors but they make for an eye-catching merger.

If theme gardens intrigue you, try planting the very late-blooming *Narcissus poeticus* var.

recurvus, a shimmering, white-petaled, red-rimmed daffodil, with *Hyacinthoides hispanica* 'White Triumphator'. Some people have said this combination resembles "moon gardening" because you can often see these white flowers at night.

Pale-colored flowers always reflect available light, and as such, they show up better if you

place them where they can shine. A white daffodil such as *Narcissus* 'Beersheba' is much more visible in the garden when planted in front of a burgundy-leafed peony. After the daffodils have finished blooming, that same peony will have beautiful magenta flowers in full glorious bloom. Plant a few bulbs of the silvery-white flowered *Allium*

Grape hyacinths (Muscari armeniacum) and the tulip 'Abba' provide a riot of spring color.

White Allium nigrum, *paired with the fuschia tones of a peony. The allium is hardy in Zones 4 to 7.*

These windflowers (Anenome cornaria de Caen) *are one of the more tender bulbs, hardy only in Zones 7 to 10.*

nigram *(multibulbosum)* next to peonies. These beauties sway neatly around the dark foliage later in the season.

You can also enjoy a theme garden with a patriotic flavor, using two white daffodils—'Ice Wings' and 'Petrel'—with the Darwin Hybrid red tulip 'Parade'. Include the blue flowers of *Muscari latifolium* and *Anemone coronaria de Caen* 'Mr. Fokker' to complete the spread. The icing on the cake is a few precious little red and white 'Lady Jane' tulips for good measure.

Terrific twosomes

The narcissus 'Saint Patrick's Day' is a favorite daffodil. It has luminous sulfur-yellow petals that surround a broad, creamy white cup that can be seen and enjoyed from a distance. Plant this beauty with a bright tulip such as 'Juan', which is orange with a yellow base and has gorgeous burgundy leaves. In addition, most daffodils are hardy in Zones 3 to 8, which means gar-

deners in most of the country can enjoy them.

The daffodil 'Ice Follies' remains another old favorite for many people, because it continues to give reliable blooms for many years. If you want to make a magnificent statement, combine

it with the popular tulip 'Red Emperor'. If you like pronounced fragrance as well as color, the dramatic daffodil 'Sir Winston Churchill' is as strong and dynamic a flower as the man for whom it was named. Put a few of these bulbs next to a contrasting colored

The tulip 'Abu Hassan'.

Snowdrop (Galanthus nivalis) *adds light to the garden in Zones 3 to 8.*

tulip like 'Abu Hassan', which is a red tulip with strong yellow edges.

If blending blossoms with similar colors appeals to you, combine the daffodil 'Yellow Cheerfulness' with an underplanting of *Anemone blanda* 'White Splendour'. ('White Splendour' is only hardy to Zone 5, however, so gardeners in Zones 3 and 4 will have to plant these next spring.) The tiny yellow center of this daisy-like, clear white anemone reflects the same yellow as the daffodil 'Yellow Cheerfulness'. It also adds a nice ground cover of ferny foliage at the base, which looks a bit like "shoes and socks" for the otherwise undressed daffodil.

The earliest blooming split corona daffodil is the yellow-cupped 'Printal'. Plant this with the tulip 'Ancilla', which, being shorter, helps it fit nicely in the same garden space. The pairing also offers a lovely mirroring of yellow and red.

Speaking of early blooming, if you have a semi-shady or shady area, the snowdrop (*Galanthus nivalis*) is an early-blooming, tiny white flower that can lighten up an otherwise dark area of the garden. It's a member of the Amaryllis family (and is pest-resistant) and combines well with other early-blooming bulbs like the spring crocus *Crocus vernus* 'Vanguard'.

Summer favorites

In late spring and early summer, it's time for a completely different batch of bulbs to take the stage. The blossoms of Asiatic lilies and alliums, with their contrasting colors, similar heights and blooming times, make them ideal bedfellows for other early-summer flowers. For instance, drumstick alliums (*Allium sphaerocephalum*) have small, dark burgundy flowers that are sometimes difficult to see in the garden. Plant them with the bright yellow lily 'Connecticut King' for an effective—and visible—courtship.

Another favorite? The lavender blooms of the popular giant allium (*Allium giganteum*) contrast beautifully with the lily 'Avignon'. The dark-colored Dutch iris 'Purple Sensation' and creamy white flowers of *Camassia leichtlinii* also bloom compatibly with sweet William and other early summer biennials. In fact, many flowers,

---

Garden Tip
Bulbs in Containers

Is your yard or garden a bit short on space? You may have considered trying to over-winter those bulbs that require a period of chilling in outdoor containers as a result.

Unfortunately, this is a gamble in most areas. It's not so much whether or not the bulbs will freeze, although in Zones 2 to 5, chances are good that they will. The real problem comes from planting in small containers that don't have enough insulation to protect the bulbs from winter's destructive freeze/thaw cycle. However, you can plant hardy bulbs in pots in the fall and bury them in a shaded mulch pile (at least 8 to 10 inches deep or even more in the coldest areas of the country). Next spring, as soon as it begins to warm up, pull back the mulch so the stems and leaves on your flowers will not turn yellow. When outdoor bulbs begin to flower in your area, you can remove your container-grown bulbs as well.

*Drumstick alliums (*A. sphaerocephalum*).*

Try These
Hardiness Chart

Bulbs hardy within a zone may be planted in fall to bloom next year. These bulbs will also come back again and again in these zones.

Name	Zones	Blooms	Source
Narcissus—			
'Beersheba'	3 to 8	Spring	2,3
'Ice Follies'	3 to 8	Spring	1,2,3,4,5,6
'Ice Wings'	4 to 9	Spring	1,2,3,6
'Petrel'	3 to 8	Spring	2,3
poeticus var. recurvus	3 to 7	Spring	2,3,5,6
'Saint Patrick's Day'	3 to 8	Spring	2,3
'Sir Winston Churchill'	3 to 9	Spring	1,2,3,4
'Yellow Cheerfulness'	3 to 9	Spring	2,3,6
Tulipa—			
'Abba'	3 to 8	Spring	2
'Abu Hassan'	3 to 8	Spring	n/a
'Ancilla'	3 to 8	Spring	2,3
'Juan'	3 to 9	Spring	2,3,6
'Lady Jane'	3 to 8	Spring	n/a
'Orange Monarch'	3 to 8	Spring	n/a
'Parade'	3 to 8	Spring	1,2
'Prinses Irene'	3 to 8	Spring	1,2,3,4,6
'Red Emperor'	3 to 9	Spring	2,3,4,5
'Temple of Beauty'	3 to 8	Spring	2,3
'White Triumpator'	3 to 8	Spring	1,2,3,4
Allium—			
giganteum	5 to 8	Spring	1,2,3,5,6
nigram	4 to 7	Spring	2,3
sphaerocephalon	5 to 8	Spring	1,2,3,5,6
Anemone—			
blanda 'White Splendour'	5 to 8	Spring	1,2,3,4,6
Coranaria de Caen 'Mr. Fokker'	7 to 10	Spring,[1]	2
Arum italicum	5 to 9	Spring	1,2,3,4
Camassia leichtlinii	3 to 8	Spring	2,3,6
Crocus vernus—			
'Vanguard'	3 to 8	Spring	2
Galanthus nivalis	3 to 8	Spring	1,2,3,4,5,6
Hyacinthoides—			
hispanica 'Excelsior'	4 to 10	Spring	2
hispanica 'White Triumphator'	4 to 10	Spring	2
Iris (Dutch)— 'Purple Sensation'	5 to 9	Late spring/ early summer	2,3
Leucojum aestivum	4 to 9	Spring	2,3,4,6
Lilium—			
'Connecticut King'	4 to 8	Summer	5,6
'Avignon'	4 to 8	Summer	n/a
Lycoris radiata	7 to 10	Summer	1,2,3,5
Muscari—			
armeniacum	4 to 9	Spring	2,3,6
latifolium	4 to 8	Spring	2,3,6

Notes
[1]Can plant in spring and dig in autumn in cool areas.

Allium giganteum *and the lily 'Avignon' are a classic summer-blooming pair. The allium is reliably hardy in Zones 5 to 8 (sometimes to Zone 4), and the lily is hardy in Zones 4 to 8.*

such as larkspur, bachelor's button, Queen Anne's lace, yarrow and violas, can be over-seeded on top of a flower bed filled with bulbs and perennials. These flowers add color and texture to the early-summer garden.

Late-season favorites

Some plants provide interest all season long. *Arum italicum* is a shade lover that is a three-season plant. It has a yellow "Jack-in-the-pulpit" type bloom in the spring, spikes of red berries all summer and dark green, beautifully variegated leaves that persist all winter. It's one of the most underutilized, special bulbs available. Each year it gets better in our Zone 7 garden.

A final favorite is *Lycoris radiata*, sometimes known as "Hurricane Lilies" or "British soldiers." This is a hardy member of the Amaryllis family, and it

Arum italicum offers wonderful ornamental berries in fall. It's hardy in Zones 5 to 9.

The fall crocus (Sternbergia lutea) is hardy in Zones 6 to 9.

blooms in early fall when there's not much else in the garden. Its red, spidery-looking flowers perch atop naked stems and last forever in a vase. They are hardy to Zone 7, but I've seen them in Zone 6, mulched in protected locations.

Spider lilies (Lycoris radiata) are also known "British soldiers." They are hardy in Zones 7 to 10.

Garden Tip
Planting Bulbs

As a good rule of thumb, most spring-blooming bulbs should be planted three times as deep as they are tall. However, I've found I have more success with tulips if they are planted deeper, so my rule for them is to plant them four times as deep as they are tall. That means a bulb that is 2 inches tall would be planted 6 inches deep for the "three-times rule" and 8 inches deep for the "four-times rule." Keeping this in mind, most tulips should be planted about 8 to 10 inches deep,

Before digging holes for your fall bulbs, arrange them on the ground to check for placement.

while most daffodils should be planted about 6 inches deep. Smaller bulbs, such as muscari and anemones, can be planted 3 to 4 inches deep.

EASY COLOR FROM BULBS

We just suggested "what" bulbs you might plant this fall. Here are the details on the "how."

Daffodils are dream bulbs for a less-work garden. They bloom beautifully year after year, and even hungry mice leave them alone.

Throughout this section, bulbs are often mentioned as low-maintenance plants that deliver lots of color for their cost, both in terms of time and money. That's because bulbs are essentially little ready-to-bloom horticultural packages. Plant them, give them a few months to root and grow and you will be rewarded with spectacular flowers year after year.

There are hundreds of species of bulbs, from tiny white snowdrops to huge drumstick alliums. Don't be afraid to try any bulb that interests you, because chances are excellent that they will do well. The most popular bulbs are described on the following pages, but there are many more worth trying.

Landscaping with Bulbs

In addition to rich, eye-catching color, bulbs have elegant forms that deserve to be admired up close. Plant bulbs in clusters so that a group of uniform blooms appears in a concentrated space. This usually looks much better than arranging bulbs in straight lines or sprinkling them through a flower bed.

Numerous bulbs fall into the category of spring-flowering bulbs. Daffodils, hyacinths and tulips lead this parade. Plant these bulbs in the fall, because they need the winter season to develop roots. And don't worry if the leaves poke through the soil before the last snow has melted. The bulbs know what they're doing. They will survive and bloom beautifully.

You can plant spring-flowering bulbs by digging a broad, flat-bottomed planting hole and arranging a number of bulbs together in the bottom or by using a tool called a bulb planter that takes up plugs of soil. Then drop the bulb in the hole, doing your best to get it right side up, and pulverize the soil plug to fill in over the bulb. If you are planting hundreds of bulbs, there are even augers you can use that attach to rechargeable drills—a fast way to speed up the job.

Summer bulbs such as lilies or gladiolus need a proper flower bed to grow their best, so take

Watch Out!
Repel Rodents

Mice and other rodents eat numerous types of bulbs, including crocus and tulips. They leave daffodils alone, so you may have some luck encircling more palatable bulbs with daffodils. Another defensive strategy is to plant bulbs in deep pots, sink the pots in the ground up to their rims, and then cover them with chicken wire. You can also fashion baskets from chicken wire and place them in the planting holes before planting the bulbs. The wire baskets are hidden from view after planting, but tunneling rodents can't get through them to devour your bulbs.

Plant tulips in the fall for an eye-catching display in mid-spring. Tulips naturalize better in cool climates than in places where summers are long and hot.

Hardy gladiolus don't grow as tall as more tender florists' types, but they can be left in the ground year-round to Zone 6.

some time preparing a suitable planting hole for them, well-amended with compost or other organic matter. Add mulch to keep the soil moist, and you have every reason to expect success.

Tips for Better Bulbs

Bulbs come with the basic equipment to grow themselves, but there are a few pointers to keep in mind to get the most out of these miraculous little packages.

- **Plant Plenty:** A dozen tulips grouped together is not too many. You may be able to use fifty little crocuses that bloom close to the ground.

- **Drainage Counts:** Bulbs can rot when grown in low places where the soil does not drain well. But because most bulbs need to be planted deeply, rotting is a constant risk in high rainfall areas. One approach that works well and looks great is to encircle a planting space with large stones, place bulbs in the bottom of the enclosure and then fill in over them with several inches of soil.

- **Chill Before Planting:** In Zones 8 and 9, it's important to refrigerate spring-flowering bulbs for up to 6 weeks before planting them in early winter. Warm soil causes them to start growing soon after planting, which can be a disaster.

- **Leave Skins Intact:** Never peel bulbs before planting them. The skins help protect them from pests and diseases.

- **Calculate Planting Depth:** Cover bulbs with soil twice as deep as the size of the bulb. Plant a 1-inch diameter bulb 3 inches deep (1 inch of bulb, 2 inches of soil on top), a 2-inch bulb 6 inches deep, and so forth. Mix a little compost into the soil under the bulb so that when the roots emerge they find some nutrition waiting for them.

- **Let the Leaves Mature:** The green season for bulb plants is when they store up supplies for the next season's bloom, so neither mow, tie, bend nor smother the leaves after the flowers are gone. Instead be patient and wait until the leaves naturally turn yellow to clean up behind your bulbs.

The skins that cover tulips and other bulbs deter rodents and keep the bulbs from sprouting until the time is right.

TREES FOR AUTUMN COLOR

Gardening isn't just for flowers! Here we reveal a wide variety of trees that are regional favorites for fall beauty from both leaves and fruit.

Persimmon tree.

Chinese pistache.

Pacific Coast

When friends from New England call people out west, they usually boast about their foliage show. That's when you can smile and think, "Why ruin their fun by describing our radiantly red Japanese maple (*Acer palmatum* 'Bloodgood', Zones 6 to 8) and persimmon tree (*Diospyros kaki* 'Fuyu', Zones 7 to 10) festooned with orange leaves and fruits, or describe a downtown surrounded by dozens of outrageously pink and orange pistache (*Pistacia chinensis*, Zones 7 to 9) street trees?" Autumn in the West can be spectacular if you choose the right trees, and these three are all-time favorites. The maple needs a fair amount of water and occasional care, but the others are somewhat drought-tolerant and generally low-maintenance.

Desert Southwest

Cottonwoods glow yellow along rivers in autumn. So some gardeners crave red leaves—to offset all of that gold. Drought-tolerant Chinese pistache (*Pistacia chinensis*, Zones 7 to 9) is a standout in red-orange and deeper shades of crimson, too. A favorite tree for interest in any season is the curl-leaf mountain mahogany (*Cercocarpus ledifolius*, Zones 5 to 10). It grows even under tough conditions, and the glossy green leaves turn bronzy red by late September. Plumy small fruits add a bit of whimsy.

Garden Tips

- Buy Japanese maples and persimmons from local nurseries or from specialty mail-order nurseries.
- Pistache trees can have orange, yellow or pink foliage. To choose the color you like best, purchase them from your local nursery in autumn while they're displaying their color.

Garden Tips

- Mulch the Chinese pistache after planting and lightly fertilize every two weeks in spring. Avoid planting it in clay soil.
- If your area experiences heavy winds, stake the slow-growing curl-leaf mountain mahogany.

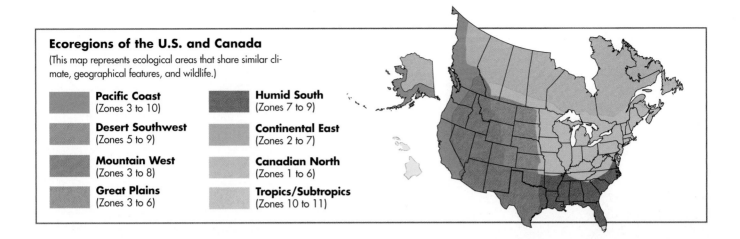

Ecoregions of the U.S. and Canada
(This map represents ecological areas that share similar climate, geographical features, and wildlife.)

Pacific Coast
(Zones 3 to 10)

Desert Southwest
(Zones 5 to 9)

Mountain West
(Zones 3 to 8)

Great Plains
(Zones 3 to 6)

Humid South
(Zones 7 to 9)

Continental East
(Zones 2 to 7)

Canadian North
(Zones 1 to 6)

Tropics/Subtropics
(Zones 10 to 11)

Russian hawthorn.

Downy serviceberry.

Mountain West

Autumn is a wonderful season because of the luminous, earthy tones abundant in the Mountain West landscape. An excellent selection is Russian hawthorn (*Crataegus ambigua*, Zones 4 to 6). This thorny, round-shaped tree will reach 25 feet tall and 20 feet wide. It has an attractive gnarly habit, and the finely cut leaves often turn yellow in autumn. The foliage plays off well when paired with the tree's bright-red fruits. Western river birch (*Betula occidentalis*, Zones 4 to 6), with its slight vaselike form, also has yellow fall color, but is a bit smaller at 15 feet tall and wide. It tolerates and even likes moist soil conditions and grows well in full sun to part shade.

Great Plains

Two favorite trees for fall color also have beautiful spring flowers. Downy serviceberry (*Amelanchier arborea*, Zones 4 to 9) grows 25 feet tall and wide, has white flowers in May, red-purple fruit in June and yellow, orange and deep-red leaves in autumn. It prefers moist, well-drained soil in full sun or partial shade. While fiery fall foliage is an asset, you will also appreciate trees with showy fruit. 'Prairifire' crabapple (*Malus* 'Prairifire', Zones 5 to 8) grows 20 feet tall and wide, is disease-resistant and has pinkish-red flowers in late April and early May. Red-purple fruit forms in the autumn and persists through winter. This tough tree grows well in full sun and average soil.

Garden Tips

- If you have young children, be careful where you plant Russian hawthorns because of the sharp thorns.
- The red berries of Russian hawthorns attract birds.

Garden Tips

- Plant trees in fall: There's less stress on plants if they are planted while the ground is warm and the air is cool. You can plant as long as the soil is not frozen.

Ginkgo.

Sugar gum.

Humid South

Lovely sourwood (*Oxydendrum arboretum*, Zones 5 to 9) slowly grows to around 50 feet tall, so its red autumn leaves and early autumn flowers aren't for every yard. But what place can't do with a statuesque Japanese maple (*Acer palmatum*, Zones 6 to 8)? 'Glowing Embers', a selection growing to about 18 feet tall, holds green leaves all summer and then blazes red-orange in autumn. For a fine finish to the season, try ancient male ginkgos (*Ginkgo biloba*, Zones 5 to 9), which often take 20 years to outgrow their awkward adolescence. Like magic, the fan-shaped leaves of gingko turn yellow all at once and then flutter down to form a golden carpet.

Continental East

Ask anyone in the East about autumn color and they'll mention the sugar maple (*Acer saccharum*, Zones 4 to 8). In mid-October, the leaves transform to a brilliant orange. It is the most important and easiest tree to grow. Transplanting easily and costing little, the secret to success is good drainage and avoiding compacted soil. On the other end of the ease spectrum is sour gum (*Nyssa sylvatica*, Zones 5 to 9). This native is the first to color and turns deep red. It has a strong taproot and is difficult to transplant. It can sulk for years after transplanting without putting on much growth. Don't fret: Buy a container-grown tree from a nursery for success.

Garden Tips

- Like many native trees, sourwoods transplant best if you purchase young, container-grown trees. Once established, they are champs at surviving drought.

- Don't overfeed Japanese maples. Too much nitrogen can make new growth weak and leggy.

Garden Tip

- If you have a small yard, look for dwarf sugar maple cultivars.

Burr oak.

Floss silk tree.

Canadian North

A pine larch (*Larix lyallii*, Zones 3 to 6) adds brilliant gold to gardens and forests each autumn. Most conifers are evergreens, but the larch drops its leaves after its dramatic color change. A native tree, it gives us northern gardeners a moment of inspiration just before the dull days of winter. North America's most northerly native oak, the burr oak (*Quercus macrocarpa*, Zones 3 to 9), grows wild from Saskatchewan to Nova Scotia. It has a taproot and deep spreading lateral roots that help it tolerate poor, dry soil and heavy winds. It has shiny orange-brown leaves in fall. If winter comes suddenly, the leaves suddenly fast-freeze brown and hang on for extended interest.

Tropics/Subtropics

Trees with autumn color in the traditional sense are relatively scarce in the semi-tropical to tropical world. Our native red maple (*Acer rubrum* 'Florida Flame', Zones 3 to 9) colors in late November with red foliage on a 40-foot tree. The native sweet gum (*Liquidamber styraciflua*, Zones 6 to 9) has colors in the red, purple and yellow range. It does well in parts of Zone 10, too. We can also get autumn color from blooms, such as the floss silk tree (*Chorisia speciosa*, Zone 10 to 11). This beauty produces 5-inch-across, dogwood-like bright-pink flowers. The thorny trunk is an identifier for this 40-foot-tall tree. Floss silk flowers in October and November.

Places to Go

- A corridor of native larches follows the high-elevation tree line along the Rocky Mountains. One of the best trails to see larch is in the Banff National Park within Alberta, just off the Trans-Canada highway on the Healy Pass Trail. It starts at the Sunshine Ski Hill parking lot, west of the Banff townsite.

- See a natural stand of burr oak in Assiniboine Forest, a large natural area park in Winnipeg, MB. Cultivated trees also line many city boulevards and adorn urban front yards.

Garden Tips

- Red maples and sweet gums do best in a moist soil location with good sunlight.

- Also consider queen crape myrtle (*Lagerstroemia speciosa*, Zones 9 to 10). It reaches 30 feet tall in Florida and has beautiful blooms of purple and pink in early summer. The large leaves turn bright red in December.

ANNUAL CUTTING GARDEN FOR FALL BOUQUETS

Fall is perfect for turning mature annuals into bouquets of beauty.

A beautiful arrangement of flowers brings the magic of the garden indoors for days of enjoyment. Celebrate with the yellow and oranges of autumn, but also use plenty of greenery to give your flower arrangements structure and depth.

When you bring flowers indoors to enjoy, you see things that you might never notice in the garden. The details of your favorite flowers become even more beautiful and exciting when you can study them up close, at eye level, whether they are part of an elaborate arrangement on your mantel or stuck in a jelly jar in your kitchen window.

To enjoy your annuals as cut flowers, you can grow them in a special backyard bed, plant them in a row of your vegetable garden or simply gather them from your front yard flower beds. Most of the best flowers for cutting need plenty of sun to develop long, straight stems and big blooms, and they're prime for cutting and arranging by early fall.

Choice Cuts

Plan for a long season of bloom and make sure to grow annuals that bloom at different times. Besides providing plenty of flowers to cut, growing different flowers helps keep your arrangements seasonal and interesting—sweet peas and bachelor buttons in spring, celosias and sunflowers in summer and gomphrena and strawflowers in late summer and fall. Choose colors that work well with your indoor décor. Include hues that match your interiors and brighter shades that provide riveting contrast. Light and bright colors are often more useful than very dark shades, which often get lost in dim indoor lighting.

Your flower-arranging possibilities will be endless if your cutting garden includes a wide range of flower forms. For example, you might use flowers that produce rounded umbels, such as ammi or trachymene, to frame the large daisy-shaped blossoms of calendula or zinnias. Flowers with a spiking form are valuable for giving arrangements strong structure. Also include soft-textured "filler" flowers such as tall ageratum and statice in your cutting garden. With all flowers grown primarily for cutting, choose

Who can sleep when a sunny breakfast nook is ready and waiting, complete with full spikes of celosia? The vibrant colors will hold in containers or can be cut for larger arrangements.

Patience does indeed have its rewards, as you will find with lisianthus. This beautiful cut flower is slow, yet not difficult, to grow. To save time, start with stocky container-grown plants in spring.

Cut flowers need fresh, clean water. To keep the water in your arrangements from being fouled with bacteria, remove all leaves that will be under water in the vase, and change the water often.

pinch or strip off all of the leaves that will be below the water level in the vase. If left intact, the low leaves will quickly rot and foul the water. Groom and arrange the stems out of strong sunlight, in a place where you can make a mess. Once an arrangement is complete, change the water every day or so to make the blooms last as long as possible.

Collecting Containers

Most of the cut flowers you grow in your yard will have stems only about 10 to 12 inches long, and they will not look right if you put them in tall, narrow bud vases intended for long-stemmed roses. As a general guideline, flower arrangements look best if the container is less than half as high as the length of the tallest stems. So, with home-grown cut flowers, you will prob-

ably find that low containers are more useful and versatile than very tall ones.

Collect bottles, jars with narrow mouths and small pitchers and vases with varying types of finishes. Elegant crystal or clear glass containers are ideal for arrangements of a single type of flower, but with mixed arrangements, it's often best to hide the stems in a solid-colored container.

If you're generous by nature (as gardeners tend to be), rescue promising-looking jars or plastic bottles from your recycling bin. When you want to share a bouquet, you can dress up something as plain as a soft drink bottle by wrapping it with tissue paper tied with a piece or raffia or ribbon.

tall varieties that have long stems rather than compact dwarf types.

The Kindest Cuts

Harvesting blossoms is actually good for many annual flowers in that it forces them to develop additional bud-bearing stems instead of expending energy nurturing seeds. Most flowers last longest in a vase if you cut them the day that they open. With flowers that grow on spiking stems, like snapdragons and salvia, cut stems when half of the blossoms along the spike have opened.

Use a sharp knife or pruning shears to cut blossoms early in the morning, when the flowers are well rested from a day in the sun and the petals are full of water. Immediately place the stems in a deep vessel of water and move them to a cool, dark place until you are ready to arrange them. It's important to

Try These
25 Fine Annuals for Cutting

Almost any annual will last in a vase for a day or two, but the flowers listed here have the best staying power in indoor arrangements. If the water level in a container of cut flowers drops overnight, it's a sign that the stems are still taking up water—the one talent needed by all good cut flowers.

Zinnias.

ageratum	larkspur
ammi	nicotiana
aster	salvia
bachelor button	scabiosa
bells of Ireland	snapdragon
black-eyed Susan	statice
calendula	stocks
celosia	strawflowers
cobbity daisy	sunflower
euphorbia	sweet pea
foxglove	trachymene
gomphrena	zinnia
grasses	

The most willing of all annual flowers for cutting, zinnias produce more blossoms the more you cut them. Blossoms last longest in arrangements when they are gathered when freshly opened.

F A L L
ENTERTAINING

Every season of the year is a good time to have family and friends over, and autumn is no exception. Frosty nights make it good to be cozy inside with good friends and a good meal. Football game gatherings in the den or family room are cause for good eating. Halloween is for more than just trick-or-treat candy (as one of our menus suggests). And of course, fall serves up the classic celebration of Thanksgiving. Here are entertaining menus for all of fall!

Facing page: Squash Bisque, page 156

KICK-OFF PARTY

With this easy, do-ahead party, there is not much to worry about on game day. Spend all your time enjoying the game or your guests ... or worrying about which topping you'll put on your steak sandwich.

Menu
~ Grilled Flank Steak
~ Blue Cheese Mushroom Topping
~ Red Onion Pickles Topping
~ Puttanesca-Style Tomato Topping
~ Game Ball Brownies

Entertains 8.

GRILLED FLANK STEAK

A rich, beefy flavor makes this flank steak a perfect choice for a steak sandwich loaded

with toppings.

2   lb. flank steak
1   teaspoon salt
1   teaspoon freshly ground pepper

1 Heat broiler.

2 Season steak with salt and pepper. Place steak on broiler pan; broil about 4 inches from heat source 3 to 4 minutes per side or until nicely browned. Remove from broiler; loosely cover with aluminum foil. Let rest about 5 minutes. Slice steak across the grain into thin slices.

Serves 8.
Preparation time: 9 minutes.
Ready to serve: 15 minutes.
Per serving: 165 calories, 7.5 g total fat (3 g saturated fat), 60 mg cholesterol, 345 mg sodium, 0 g fiber.

Before the Event

Make the beef ahead, slice and serve cold.

Menu Tip

• Grilled Flank Steak is an excellent choice for beef lovers who are not fond of the meat's high fat content. Flank steak is very flavorful, but also very lean. Since it is also one of the toughest cuts of meat, it is important to remember to cut it across the grain in thin slices.

BLUE CHEESE MUSHROOM TOPPING

If you haven't tasted the combination of mushrooms and blue cheese, you are in for a treat. This combo for fall even sways people who swear they don't like blue cheese.

2   tablespoons butter
1   lb. fresh mushrooms, sliced
½   teaspoon salt
¼   teaspoon freshly ground pepper
4   oz. blue cheese, crumbled

1 In large saucepan, heat butter over medium-high heat until melted. Add mushrooms; cook, stirring occasionally, until brown, about 8 minutes. Season with salt and pepper. Add blue cheese; continue cooking until cheese is melted.

Serves 8.
Preparation time: 10 minutes.
Ready to serve: 20 minutes.
Per serving: 90 calories, 7 g total fat (4.5 g saturated fat), 20 mg cholesterol, 365 mg sodium, 1 g fiber.

Before the Event
Prepare this topping one day ahead, refrigerate and warm just before serving.

RED ONION PICKLES TOPPING

The combination of onions and beef is a match made in heaven. These hot onion pickles add a new twist to an old favorite.

1   large red onion
¾   cup rice vinegar
⅓   cup sugar
1   teaspoon crushed red pepper

1 Peel and cut onion into ½-inch slices; separate rings.

2 In medium skillet, heat vinegar, sugar and crushed red pepper over medium heat about 1 minute or until sugar dissolves. Add onion rings to skillet; toss to coat. Cook about 2 minutes or until onions wilt.

Serves 8.
Preparation time: 5 minutes.
Ready to serve: 10 minutes.
Per serving: 45 calories, 0 g total fat (0 g saturated fat), 0 mg cholesterol, 2 mg sodium, 0 g fiber.

Before the Event
Prepare this topping one day ahead, refrigerate and warm them just before serving.

PUTTANESCA-STYLE TOMATO TOPPING

Anchovies add a distinct but subtle flavor to this earthy autumn tomato sauce.

2   (14.5-oz.) cans diced tomatoes with garlic
    and onions
½   cup chopped pitted ripe olives
¼   cup capers
2   anchovy fillets, minced

1 In large saucepan, combine tomatoes, olives, capers and anchovies; bring to a simmer over medium heat, stirring occasionally. Simmer mixture about 5 minutes or until it thickens and the flavors have blended.

Serves 8.
Preparation time: 5 minutes.
Ready to serve: 10 minutes.
Per serving: 45 calories, 1 g total fat (0 g saturated fat), 1 mg cholesterol, 500 mg sodium, 1 g fiber.

Before the Event

Prepare this topping one day ahead, refrigerate and warm just before serving.

GAME BALL BROWNIES

This brownie football makes a tempting dessert and doubles as a clever centerpiece as well. Another bonus: The host can snack on the pieces he or she removed to make the football shape.

1 (15.5-oz.) pkg. brownie mix
1 cup prepared milk chocolate frosting (from 16-oz. can)
1 tube yellow decorator frosting

Before the Event
Make, bake and decorate *Game Ball Brownies* a day ahead.

1 Prepare brownie mix according to package directions. Pour mixture into 9-inch square pan lined with aluminum foil and coated with nonstick cooking spray. Bake according to package directions.

2 When brownies have baked and cooled, turn onto platter; remove foil. With knife, remove corners to create an oval that resembles a football.

3 Frost brownie with milk chocolate frosting. Create football laces with yellow frosting.

Serves 8.
Preparation time: 20 minutes.
Ready to serve: 40 minutes.
Per serving: 350 calories, 19 g total fat (12 g saturated fat), 35 mg cholesterol, 10 mg sodium, 2 g fiber.

Autumn Dinner Party

There is color in the trees, a chill in the air and friends to entertain. This perfect fall menu warms the heart (and taste buds!) as the temperature and leaves fall.

Menu

~ Squash Bisque
~ Classic Caponata
~ Mustard-Crusted Lamb Chops
~ Yukon Gold Mashed Potatoes
~ Rustic Apple Tart

Entertains 8.

SQUASH BISQUE

This rich and creamy autumn soup tastes like it took hours of work. But it really only takes a few easy minutes!

1½ lb. peeled, cooked winter squash
3   tablespoons packed brown sugar
1   cup reduced-sodium chicken broth
¾   cup cream
¼   cup sherry
½   teaspoon salt
⅛   teaspoon freshly ground pepper

1 In medium-large saucepan, combine squash, brown sugar, chicken broth, cream and sherry; bring to a simmer over medium heat.

2 Season with salt and pepper. Simmer 10 minutes or until flavors are blended.

Serves 8.
Preparation time: 5 minutes.
Ready to serve: 15 minutes.
Per serving: 125 calories, 7.5 g total fat (4.5 g saturated fat), 25 mg cholesterol, 215 mg sodium, 2.5 g fiber.

Before the Event

Make *Squash Bisque* a day ahead. Cool, cover and refrigerate, then warm before serving.

CLASSIC CAPONATA

Choosing the right eggplant makes all the difference in the success of this dish. Look for an autumn eggplant with shiny, unblemished skin that feels heavy for its size. This usually designates a male eggplant that has fewer seeds; it is often the seeds that give an eggplant bitterness.

3	tablespoons olive oil
1½	lb. eggplant, peeled, diced
1	cup chopped onions
¼	cup balsamic vinegar
1	(14.5-oz.) can diced tomatoes
1	(4.5-oz.) can sliced ripe olives, drained
⅓	cup pine nuts
3	tablespoons capers

1 In large skillet, heat oil over medium-high heat until hot. Add eggplant and onions; cook until onions are soft and eggplant is brown, about 5 minutes, stirring frequently.

2 Add vinegar, tomatoes, olives, pine nuts and capers; bring to a boil. Reduce heat to medium-low; simmer, stirring occasionally, 15 minutes.

Serves 8.
Preparation time: 5 minutes.
Ready to serve: 30 minutes.
Per serving: 125 calories, 9.5 g total fat (1.5 g saturated fat), 0 mg cholesterol, 280 mg sodium, 3.5 g fiber.

Before the Event

Create *Classic Caponata* a day ahead, then cover and refrigerate until you're ready to serve.

MUSTARD-CRUSTED LAMB CHOPS

A great deal of our lamb meat comes from Australia, which means we can enjoy spring lamb in the fall. This dish also works wonderfully with pork chops.

16 (5-oz.) loin lamb chops, about ¾ inch thick
¼ cup coarse-grain mustard
4 cups fresh bread crumbs
3 tablespoons olive oil

Before the Event

Bread crumbs can be made a day ahead. The chops can be coated earlier in the day, then covered and refrigerated until you're ready to cook.

1 Heat oven to 375°F.

2 Coat lamb chops evenly with mustard; press chops into bread crumbs.

3 In large skillet, heat 1½ tablespoons of the oil over high heat. Add 8 of the chops; sear, turning once, about 4 minutes or until brown. Transfer chops to large rimmed baking sheet. Repeat with remaining chops.

4 Bake about 10 minutes or to desired doneness.

Serves 8.
Preparation time: 10 minutes.
Ready to serve: 30 minutes.
Per serving: 330 calories, 16.5 g total fat (4.5 g saturated fat), 105 mg cholesterol, 280 mg sodium, 0.5 g fiber.

YUKON GOLD MASHED POTATOES

Fall's Yukon Gold potatoes display a golden buttery look. Combined with their creamy taste, they're perfect candidates for mashing.

3 lb. Yukon Gold potatoes, peeled, diced
¼ cup (½ stick) unsalted butter
½ cup milk, heated
¼ cup sour cream
1 tablespoon prepared horseradish
¾ teaspoon salt
¼ teaspoon freshly ground pepper

1 In 3-quart saucepan, cover potatoes with cold water. Bring water to a boil over medium-high heat. Reduce heat to medium-low. Simmer potatoes about 20 minutes or until tender. Remove pan from heat. Drain potatoes thoroughly.

2 Return potatoes to saucepan; mash. Add butter, hot milk, sour cream, horseradish, salt and pepper. Continue mashing until smooth.

Before the Event

Make *Yukon Gold Mashed Potatoes* ahead of time and place in a casserole for reheating at 350°F for 30 minutes.

Serves 8.
Preparation time: 10 minutes.
Ready to serve: 35 minutes.
Per serving: 205 calories, 7.5 g total fat (4.5 g saturated fat), 20 mg cholesterol, 275 mg sodium, 3 g fiber.

RUSTIC APPLE TART

This tart is so simple yet so wonderful. Golden Delicious apples are perfect because they cook quickly and the slices hold their shape.

Pastry Dough

1½   cups all-purpose flour
½   cup (1 stick) unsalted butter, cold and cut
        into slices
¼   teaspoon salt
⅓   cup very cold water

Filling

2   medium Golden Delicious apples, peeled,
        cored, thinly sliced
¼   cup sugar
1   teaspoon ground cinnamon

Before the Event

Prepare *Rustic Apple Tart* a day ahead and refrigerate. Warm before serving.

1 In bowl, mix flour, butter and salt very lightly with pastry blender, so that butter pieces remain visible throughout flour. Add cold water; mix very quickly until dough coheres. Form into round; wrap with plastic wrap. Refrigerate 30 minutes.

2 Heat oven to 400°F.

3 Roll dough to form 10-inch circle. Place on large baking sheet.

4 Top dough with apple slices, leaving 1-inch border. Sprinkle apples with sugar and cinnamon. Fold border up over apples; pinch into place.

5 Bake 25 minutes or until crust is golden brown.

Serves 8.
Preparation time: 40 minutes.
Ready to serve: 1 hour, 5 minutes.
Per serving: 225 calories, 13 g total fat (3 g saturated fat), 0 mg cholesterol, 180 mg sodium, 1 g fiber.

TAKE IT EASY THIS FALL

This is a first-rate impromptu "TGIF" supper, but it also works any time you just want to kick back with friends. It's fast and easy and a real treat after a long week ... or a day outside on an autumn hike.

Menu

~ Mediterranean Pizza
~ Salsa Shrimp with Feta
~ Couscous with Pine Nuts
~ Warm Ginger Pineapple Sauce on Vanilla Ice Cream

Entertains 4.

MEDITERRANEAN PIZZA

This pizza looks as beautiful as it tastes. Keep a good prebaked crust on hand for this quick appetizer.

1   (12-inch) prebaked pizza crust
2   cups (8 oz.) shredded mozzarella cheese
2   cups chopped fresh spinach
½   cup pitted kalamata olives, chopped
½   cup red onion slices
1   tomato, seeded, chopped or 8 cherry tomatoes, sliced
1   teaspoon crushed red pepper

1 Heat oven to 400°F.

2 Sprinkle pizza crust with 1 cup of the mozzarella. Add spinach, olives, red onion, tomato and crushed red pepper.

3 Top with remaining 1 cup mozzarella. Place crust on large baking sheet. Bake about 10 minutes or until cheese melts and toppings are warmed through.

Serves 4.
Preparation time: 15 minutes.
Ready to serve: 25 minutes.
Per serving: 375 calories, 15.5 g total fat (7 g saturated fat), 30 mg cholesterol, 780 mg sodium, 3 g fiber.

Before the Event

Assemble *Mediterranean Pizza* earlier in the day, but bake at mealtime.

SALSA SHRIMP WITH FETA

Making a salsa that suits your taste is well worth the effort. Everything in this recipe

cooks in a snap, creating a dish that bursts with homemade flavor.

2 tablespoons olive oil
1¼ lb. shelled, deveined uncooked large shrimp
2 medium zucchini, sliced
1½ cups salsa
4 oz. feta cheese, crumbled

Before the Event

Cook shrimp through the day ahead and refrigerate.

1 In large saucepan, heat oil over medium-high heat until hot. Add shrimp; sauté about 1 minute or until shrimp just turn pink and are firm. Add zucchini; sauté an additional minute. Add salsa to saucepan; cook about 1 minute or until mixture is heated through but zucchini is still crisp-tender. Top with feta.

Serves 4.
Preparation time: 5 minutes.
Ready to serve: 10 minutes.
Per serving: 270 calories, 14 g total fat (5.5 g saturated fat), 230 mg cholesterol, 800 mg sodium, 3 g fiber.

COUSCOUS WITH PINE NUTS

Couscous is really parcooked semolina pasta. It's hard to believe that it was once considered exotic! The 5-minute cooking time is a real asset to quick-cooking needs.

1   tablespoon butter
1   cup couscous
¼   cup pine nuts
2   cups reduced-sodium chicken broth

Before the Event

Prepare a day ahead. Microwave for 1 minute at High to warm through.

1 In medium skillet, heat butter over medium-high heat until melted. Add couscous and pine nuts; sauté 1 minute.

2 Meanwhile, in small saucepan, bring chicken broth to a boil over medium heat. Pour chicken broth into skillet; cover and turn off heat. Let stand 5 minutes; uncover and fluff with fork.

Serves 4.
Preparation time: 5 minutes.
Ready to serve: 10 minutes.
Per serving: 260 calories, 8.5 g total fat (2.5 g saturated fat), 10 mg cholesterol, 270 mg sodium, 3 g fiber.

WARM GINGER PINEAPPLE SAUCE ON VANILLA ICE CREAM

Use almost any quick-cooking fruit (such as bananas or pears) in this sauce and it will still taste delicious.

¼ cup (½ stick) butter
½ cup packed dark brown sugar
¼ cup pineapple juice
1 tablespoon minced fresh ginger
2 cups diced fresh pineapple
1 pint vanilla ice cream

1 In medium skillet, heat butter over medium heat until melted. Add brown sugar, pineapple juice and ginger, stirring until combined. Add pineapple; cook about 1 minute or until heated through. Serve warm over ice cream.

Serves 4.
Preparation time: 10 minutes.
Ready to serve: 15 minutes.
Per serving: 390 calories, 19 g total fat (11.5 g saturated fat), 60 mg cholesterol, 140 mg sodium, 1 g fiber.

Before the Event
Make the pineapple sauce ahead and warm it at the last minute.

A Very Scary Affair

Don't be frightened! It is easy to throw a Halloween party that will amuse young and old alike. This menu may look spooky, but everything tastes just swell.

Menu

~ Bat Chips and Salsa
~ Bread Stick Bones
~ White Chocolate Pretzel Ghosts
~ Creepy Baked Apples
~ Halloween Ravioli with Red Pepper Sauce

Entertains 8.

BAT CHIPS AND SALSA

It is easy to find all kinds of Halloween cookie cutters, bats included, in the grocery store.

8 (10-inch) flour tortillas
3 tablespoons olive oil
½ cup shredded Parmesan cheese
1 jar prepared salsa

1 Heat oven to 375°F.

2 Cut tortillas into bat shapes using cookie cutter or scissors. With pastry brush, coat each "bat" evenly with olive oil; sprinkle with Parmesan cheese.

3 Place "bats" on large ungreased baking sheet. Bake about 10 minutes or until tortillas are crisp. Serve with your favorite salsa.

Serves 8.
Preparation time: 15 minutes.
Ready to serve: 30 minutes.
Per serving: 300 calories, 11.5 g total fat (2.5 g saturated fat), 5 mg cholesterol, 600 mg sodium, 3 g fiber.

Before the Event

Make the *Bat Chips* earlier in the day.

CREEPY BAKED APPLES

It doesn't take a lot of work to make an everyday baked apple look creepy. You just have to start with one of fall's yellow or green apples, sweeten it with a blood-red jam and, of course, make it wormy!

8   Golden Delicious apples
1½   cups strawberry jam
16   gummy worms

Before the Event

Prepare the apples earlier in the day, but bake just before serving.

1 Heat oven to 350°F.

2 Core apples from the top, but not all the way through to the bottom. Fill each hole with about 1½ tablespoons strawberry jam. Place apples in ungreased 13x9-inch pan. Bake 30 minutes or until tender.

3 Remove apples from oven; cool. Add more jam; place gummy worms evenly around each apple.

Serves 8.
Preparation time: 5 minutes.
Ready to serve: 35 minutes.
Per serving: 255 calories, 5 g total fat (0 g saturated fat), 30 mg cholesterol, 30 mg sodium, 4.5 g fiber.

Halloween Ravioli with Red Pepper Sauce

Orange sauce and black olives comprise the perfect color scheme for spooky festivities. A jar of roasted red peppers is a must in every pantry, as it has so many uses.

2   tablespoons butter
1   medium onion, chopped
1   (12-oz.) jar roasted red bell peppers, drained
1   (8-oz.) container sour cream
2   (9-oz.) pkg. cheese ravioli, cooked according
      to package directions
1   cup sliced ripe olives
1   cup freshly grated Parmesan cheese

Before the Event
Create the *Red Pepper Sauce* a day ahead of time and heat before serving.

1 In medium skillet, heat butter over medium-high heat until melted. Add onion; sauté about 5 minutes or until tender.

2 Place sautéed onion, roasted peppers and sour cream in blender; puree until smooth. Pour mixture into skillet; heat over medium heat without bringing it to a boil. Cook, covered, 5 minutes.

3 Serve sauce over cooked ravioli. Top with olives and Parmesan cheese.

Serves 8.
Preparation time: 10 minutes.
Ready to serve: 15 minutes.
Per serving: 290 calories, 19.5 g total fat (10 g saturated fat), 100 mg cholesterol, 1255 mg sodium, 1 g fiber.

JUST DUCKY DINNER

You don't have to be a hunter to know that fall is the perfect season for delicious duck. This dinner menu combines many of fall's other great tastes.

Menu

~ Smoked Salmon Pâté
~ Sautéed Duck Breasts with Balsamic Sauce
~ Hazelnut-Crusted Goat Cheese Rounds with Mixed Greens
~ Hazelnut Vinaigrette
~ Baked Sweet Potato Spears
~ Roasted Pears with Sherry Apricot Sauce

Entertains 6.

SMOKED SALMON PÂTÉ

This pâté is easy to make and delivers a wonderful smoky taste that says "autumn!"

Pate

4.5	oz. heat-smoked salmon, skin removed, finely chopped
1	(8-oz.) pkg. cream cheese, room temperature
¼	cup diced red onion
2	tablespoons capers
¼	teaspoon lemon juice

Bread

24	slices miniature pumpernickel bread

Topping

1	English cucumber, thinly sliced

1 In medium bowl, combine salmon, cream cheese, red onion, capers and lemon juice; mix well.

2 Spread salmon mixture evenly over each slice of bread. Top each with 1 slice cucumber.

Serves 6.
Preparation time: 15 minutes.
Ready to serve: 25 minutes.
Per serving: 240 calories, 15 g total fat (8.5 g saturated fat), 45 mg cholesterol, 540 mg sodium, 2.5 g fiber.

Before the Event

Make *Smoked Salmon Pâté* one day ahead.

SAUTÉED DUCK BREASTS WITH BALSAMIC SAUCE

Ducks are notorious for being fatty, messy to cook and difficult to eat. Boned skinless duck breasts deliver rich taste without any of the hazards. Cook breasts to medium with a pink interior, but a slightly longer cooking time will accommodate guests who prefer their duck well done.

6	boneless skinless duck breasts
2	tablespoons olive oil
3	tablespoons sugar
1	tablespoon water
3	tablespoons balsamic vinegar
1	cup reduced-sodium chicken broth

Before the Event

Cook duck breasts earlier in the day and refrigerate them. Slice and add to the reduced sauce to warm through.

1 Pat duck breasts dry. In large skillet, heat oil over medium-high heat until hot. Add duck breasts; sauté 10 minutes, turning once, until juice runs pink. Remove each breast to paper towel; loosely cover with aluminum foil to keep warm. Let rest 5 minutes.

2 Add sugar to skillet, allowing it to melt and turn golden, about 1 minute. Add water and vinegar, stirring constantly. Add chicken broth; bring to a boil and reduce by half, about 5 minutes.

3 Holding sharp knife at 45-degree angle, slice each breast into ¼-inch slices. Fan slices on serving plate. Serve with sauce.

Serves 6.
Preparation time: 15 minutes.
Ready to serve: 20 minutes.
Per serving: 210 calories, 12 g total fat (3.5 g saturated fat), 60 mg cholesterol, 125 mg sodium, 0 g fiber.

HAZELNUT-CRUSTED GOAT CHEESE ROUNDS WITH MIXED GREENS

"Irresistible" is what they'll say about the warm rounds of nut-crusted cheese on cool and crisp greens. Top with *Hazelnut Vinaigrette* (page 183).

½ cup finely chopped toasted hazelnuts*
½ cup fresh bread crumbs
6 oz. mild goat cheese
8 cups mixed greens

Menu Tip

* To toast hazelnuts, spread on baking sheet; bake at 375°F about 10 minutes or until lightly browned. Cool.

Before the Event

Form the cheese rounds and let them crust over the day before, then cover with plastic wrap and refrigerate.

1 Heat broiler. Line baking sheet with aluminum foil.

2 In small bowl, combine hazelnuts and bread crumbs. Place hazelnut mixture on one sheet of parchment paper. With dental floss, slice cheese into 12 portions; form into rounds. Press both sides of rounds into hazelnut mixture.

3 Place rounds on baking sheet. Place under broiler about 1 minute or until lightly toasted. Turn and toast an additional minute.

4 Arrange greens on 6 plates; place 2 rounds of goat cheese on each. Serve with *Hazelnut Vinaigrette*.

Serves 6.
Preparation time: 20 minutes.
Ready to serve: 25 minutes.
Per serving: 335 calories, 31.5 g total fat (6.5 g saturated fat), 25 mg cholesterol, 165 mg sodium, 2.5 g fiber.

HAZELNUT VINAIGRETTE

Add distinction to a simple vinaigrette with specialty oil and vinegar.

¼ cup olive oil
¼ cup hazelnut oil
3 tablespoons sherry vinegar
1 tablespoon Dijon mustard
2 teaspoons honey

1 In small bowl, whisk olive and hazelnut oils, vinegar, mustard and honey until combined.

Serves 6.
Preparation time: 5 minutes.
Ready to serve: 5 minutes.
Per serving: 170 calories, 18 g total fat (2 g saturated fat), 0 mg cholesterol, 30 mg sodium, 0 g fiber.

Before the Event
Mix *Hazelnut Vinaigrette* one day ahead.

BAKED SWEET POTATO SPEARS

Fall is most definitely sweet potato time. A browned exterior and a smooth-and-creamy center make these spears a delight of contrasting texture. Plus, sweet potatoes cook in half the time of a whole baked potato.

6 medium sweet potatoes
¼ cup (½ stick) butter, melted
1 teaspoon kosher (coarse) salt
1 teaspoon freshly ground pepper

Before the Event
Sweet potatoes can be sliced earlier in the day.

1 Heat oven to 425°F.

2 Cut each potato into 8 spears. Place spears on large baking sheet. With pastry brush, evenly coat spears with butter. Sprinkle with salt and pepper.

3 Bake 25 minutes or until golden.

Serves 6.
Preparation time: 5 minutes.
Ready to serve: 30 minutes.
Per serving: 185 calories, 8 g total fat (5 g saturated fat), 20 mg cholesterol, 320 mg sodium, 3.5 g fiber.

ROASTED PEARS WITH SHERRY APRICOT SAUCE

There is nothing more delicious than a ripe pear, and fall is the best time to find the sweetest fruit. Buy pears you know are ripe, or get them at least four days before you want to use them, to be sure they get to proper ripeness.

4	ripe firm pears, peeled, cored, sliced
¼	cup (½ stick) butter, cut into small pieces
½	cup apricot preserves
¼	cup sherry

1 Heat oven to 425°F.

2 Arrange pears in shallow baking dish; dot with butter.

3 In small bowl, combine apricot preserves and sherry. Pour mixture over pears. Bake 20 minutes or until pears turn light golden brown. Serve warm.

Serves 6.
Preparation time: 10 minutes.
Ready to serve: 30 minutes.
Per serving: 205 calories, 8 g total fat (4.5 g saturated fat), 20 mg cholesterol, 60 mg sodium, 3 g fiber.

Before the Event
Bake the pears a day ahead, refrigerate and warm through before serving.

INDEX

A

Allium, 131–133
Amaryllis, 133
An Easy Autumn To-Do List, 128–129
Anemone, 116, 132, 133
Annual Cutting Garden for Fall Bouquets, 142–143
Annuals
   drying everlasting annuals, 120–121
   for fall bouquets, 142–143
Antique Potpourri Jar, 80–82
Appetizers
   Bat Chips and Salsa, 172
   Mexican Copanata, 14
   Smoked Salmon Pâté, 180
Apple Cream Cheese Bars, 46
Apple Date Pecan Cake with Caramel Sauce, 42
Apples
   Apple Cream Cheese Bars, 46
   Apple Date Pecan Cake with Caramel Sauce, 42
   Creepy Baked Apples, 176
   Dried Apple Garland, 94–96
   Pork Chops with Dried-Apple Stuffing, 36
   Red and White Endive Slaw with Walnuts and Apples, 29
   Rustic Apple Tart, 161
Asters, 116–117
Autumn Dinner Party, 154–161
   Classic Caponata, 158
   Mustard-Crusted Lamb Chops, 159
   Rustic Apple Tart, 161
   Squash Bisque, 156
   Yukon Gold Mashed Potatoes, 160
Autumn Glory: Wildflower Gardens, 122–125
Autumn Knot Garden, 114–115
Autumn's Everlasting Annuals, 120–121

B

Bacon
   Turkey Club with Cranberry and BLT, 33
Baked Sweet Potato Spears, 184
Barley
   Root Vegetable and Barley Soup, 25
Bars
   Apple Cream Cheese Bars, 46

   Game Ball Brownies, 153
   Inside-Out Fig Bars, 43
Baskets
   Nature's Bounty Basket, 59–61
Bat Chips and Salsa, 172
Beef
   Grilled Flank Steak, 148
Beets and Oranges, 19
Birdhouse Shoe Rack, 83–87
Blue Cheese Mushroom Topping, 150
Boltonia, 117
Bread Stick Bones, 174
Brown-Ale Shiitake Mushroom Chicken, 35
Bugbane, 117
Bulbs
   allium, 131–133
   colorful combinations for, 130–132
   in containers, 133
   crocus, 133
   daffodils, 131–133, 137
   garlic, 128
   hardiness chart for, 133
   landscaping with, 136–137
   late-season favorites, 134–135
   lily, 133
   planting in fall, 130–133
   planting tips, 135
   repelling rodents, 136
   for shade, 137
   snowdrop, 133
   spider lily, 133–134
   summer favorites, 133–134
   terrific twosomes, 132–133
   tips for better, 137
   tulips, 131–133

C

Caesar Salad, 26
Cakes
   Apple Date Pecan Cake with Caramel Sauce, 42
   Pumpkin Swirl Cheesecake, 45
Canadian North region
   trees for fall color, 141
Candles and lights
   Etched Glass Candle Holder and Decorative Candle, 106–108
   Java Fire Starter, 50–52
   Wire Luminaria, 71–73

Witch Mobile, 100–102
Centerpiece
   Fall Leaf Clay Pot, 74–75
   Pumpkin Container with Mum Plant, 97–99
Cheese
   Apple Cream Cheese Bars, 46
   Blue Cheese Mushroom Topping, 150
   Figs with Cheese, Honey and Walnuts, 13
   Hazelnut-Crusted Goat Cheese Rounds with Mixed Greens, 182
   Pumpkin Swirl Cheesecake, 45
   Salsa Shrimp with Feta, 166
Chicken
   Brown-Ale Shiitake Mushroom Chicken, 35
   Fajita Chicken in Pumpkin-Seed Sauce, 34
   Honey-Sesame Chicken Tenderloins, 11
   Roast Chicken, 38
Classic Caponata, 158
Clematis, sweet autumn, 117
Cold frames, 126
Continental East region
   trees for fall color, 140
Corn Bread, 18
Couscous with Pine Nuts, 167
Crafts and decorating
   Antique Potpourri Jar, 80–82
   Birdhouse Shoe Rack, 83–87
   Dried Apple Garland, 94–96
   Etched Glass Candle Holder and Decorative Candle, 106–108
   Fall Balsam Wreath, 56–58
   Fall Chair Dressing, 109–111
   Fallen Leaves Table Topper, 103–105
   Fall Guest Hand Towel, 91–93
   Fall Leaf Clay Pot, 74–75
   Fall Leaf Stationary, 53–55
   Framed and Pressed Fall-Colored Leaves, 88–90
   Halloween Trick-or-Treat Bag, 65–67
   Java Fire Starter, 50–52
   Mini-Kindling Box, 62–64
   Nature's Bounty Basket, 59–61
   Pumpkin Container with Mum Plant, 97–99
   Red Twig Dogwood Bush, 76–77
   Scarecrow Wall Hanging, 68–70
   Wire Luminaria, 71–73

Witch Mobile, 100–102
Cranberries
 Thanksgiving Salad, 21
 Turkey Club with Cranberry and BLT, 33
Creepy Baked Apples, 176
Crocus, 133
Curried Pilaf Salad, 28
Cutting garden, 142–143

D

Daffodils, 131–133, 137
Dates
 Apple Date Pecan Cake with Caramel Sauce, 42
Decorating. *See* Crafts and decorating
Desert southwest region
 trees for fall color, 138
Desserts
 Apple Cream Cheese Bars, 46
 Apple Date Pecan Cake with Caramel Sauce, 42
 Game Ball Brownies, 153
 Inside-Out Fig Bars, 43
 Pumpkin Swirl Cheesecake, 45
 Roasted Pears with Sherry Apricot Sauce, 185
 Rustic Apple Tart, 161
 Warm Ginger Pineapple Sauce on Vanilla Ice Cream, 168
 White Chocolate Pretzel Ghosts, 175
Dips and spreads
 Blue Cheese Mushroom Topping, 150
 Mexican Copanata, 14
 Puttanesca-Style Tomato Topping, 152
 Red Onion Pickles Topping, 150
Dressing/vinaigrette
 Caesar Salad, 26
 Hazelnut Vinaigrette, 183
 Hot Pastrami Salad, 41
 Red and White Endive Slaw with Walnuts and Apples, 29
Dried Apple Garland, 94–96
Duck
 Sautéed Duck Breasts with Balsamic Sauce, 181

E

Easy Color from Bulbs, 136–137
Eggplant
 Classic Caponata, 158
Entertaining
 Autumn Dinner Party, 154–161
 Just Ducky Dinner, 178–185

Kick-Off Party, 146–153
 Take It Easy This Fall, 162–168
 A Very Scary Affair, 170–177
Etched Glass Candle Holder and Decorative Candle, 106–108

F

Fabric crafts
 Fall Chair Dressing, 109–111
 Fallen Leaves Table Topper, 103–105
 Fall Guest Hand Towel, 91–93
 Halloween Trick-or-Treat Bag, 65–67
 Scarecrow Wall Hanging, 68–70
Fajita Chicken in Pumpkin-Seed Sauce, 34
Fall Balsam Wreath, 56–58
Fall Chair Dressing, 109–111
Fallen Leaves Table Topper, 103–105
Fall Guest Hand Towel, 91–93
Fall Leaf Clay Pot, 74–75
Fall Leaf Stationary, 53–55
Fennel and Pear Salad, 31
Fertilizer
 for lawns in fall, 128
Figs
 Figs with Cheese, Honey and Walnuts, 13
 Inside-Out Fig Bars, 43
Figs with Cheese, Honey and Walnuts, 13
Fire starter
 Java Fire Starter, 50–52
Fish and Seafood
 Lox and Bagel Salad, 10
 Salsa Shrimp with Feta, 166
 Smoked Salmon Pâté, 180
Floating row cover, 126–127
Flowers, dried
 Antique Potpourri Jar, 80–82
 Dried Apple Garland, 94–96
 drying everlastings step-by-step, 120–121
 Fall Chair Dressing, 109–111
 Framed and Pressed Fall-Colored Leaves, 88–90
 making own potpourri, 121
 pressed flowers, 120
 Red Twig Dogwood Bush, 76–77
Framed and Pressed Fall-Colored Leaves, 88–90

G

Game Ball Brownies, 153
Gardening
 Annual Cutting Garden for Fall Bouquets, 142–143

Autumn Glory: Wildflower Gardens, 122–125
 Autumn Knot Garden, 114–115
 Autumn's Everlasting Annuals, 120–121
 bringing plants inside for winter, 129
 cutting garden for fall flowers, 142–143
 drying everlastings step-by-step, 120–121
 An Easy Autumn To-Do List, 128–129
 Easy Color from Bulbs, 136–137
 fall soil prep tip, 129
 knot garden, 114–115
 Late-Season Stunners, 116–119
 perennials for late-season blooming, 117–119
 planting bulbs in fall, 130–133
 Plant Now for Season-Long Bloom, 130–135
 pressed flowers, 120
 Six Ways to Extend Your Veggie-Growing Season, 126–127
 Trees for Autumn Color, 138–141
 vegetable gardens, 126–127
 wildflower gardens, 122–125
Garlic, planting in fall, 128
Geranium, 117
Glassware
 Antique Potpourri Jar, 80–82
 Etched Glass Candle Holder and Decorative Candle, 106–108
Globe Thistle, 117–118
Goldenrod, 118
Great Plains region
 trees for fall color, 139
Grilled Flank Steak, 148

H

Halloween Ravioli with Red Pepper Sauce, 177
Halloween Trick-or-Treat Bag, 65–67
Harvest "Thyme" Squash Soup, 23
Hazelnut-Crusted Goat Cheese Rounds with Mixed Greens, 182
Hazelnut Vinaigrette, 183
Helenium, 118
Helianthus, 118
Herbed Tomato Gratin, 24
Honey-Sesame Chicken Tenderloins, 11
Hot Pastrami Salad, 41

I

Inside-Out Fig Bars, 43

J

Java Fire Starter, 50–52
Joy Pye Weed, 118–119
Just Ducky Dinner, 178–185
  Baked Sweet Potato Spears, 184
  Hazelnut-Crusted Goat Cheese Rounds
    with Mixed Greens, 182
  Hazelnut Vinaigrette, 183
  Roasted Pears with Sherry Apricot
    Sauce, 185
  Sautéed Duck Breasts with Balsamic
    Sauce, 181
  Smoked Salmon Pâté, 180

K

Kick-Off Party, 146–153
  Blue Cheese Mushroom Topping, 150
  Game Ball Brownies, 153
  Grilled Flank Steak, 148
  Puttanesca-Style Tomato Topping, 152
  Red Onion Pickles Topping, 150
Knot garden, 114–115
Kugel
Savory Noodle Kugel, 20

L

Lamb
  Mustard-Crusted Lamb Chops, 159
Late-Season Stunners, 116–119
Lawns
fall fertilizing, 128
Lily, 133
Lilyturf, 119
Lox and Bagel Salad, 10

M

Marinade
  Honey-Sesame Chicken Tenderloins,
    11
Mediterranean Pizza, 164
Mexican Copanata, 14
Mini-Kindling Box, 62–64
Mobiles
  Witch Mobile, 100–102
Mountain West region
  trees for fall color, 139
Mulch, plastic, 127
Mums, 114–115
Mushrooms
  Blue Cheese Mushroom Topping, 150
  Brown-Ale Shiitake Mushroom
    Chicken, 35

Mustard-Crusted Lamb Chops, 159

N

Narcissus, 131
Nature's Bounty Basket, 59–61
North Central States
  wildflowers for, 125
Northwest region
  wildflowers for, 125
Nuts
  Apple Date Pecan Cake with Caramel
    Sauce, 42
  Figs with Cheese, Honey and Walnuts,
    13
  Hazelnut-Crusted Goat Cheese Rounds
    with Mixed Greens, 182
  Red and White Endive Slaw with
    Walnuts and Apples, 29

O

Onions
  Red Onion Pickles Topping, 150
Oranges
  Beets and Oranges, 19
  Turkey with Spinach Tortellini and
    Fresh Oranges, 40

P

Pacific Coast region
  trees for fall color, 138
Painting
  Fall Leaf Clay Pot, 74–75
Paper crafts
  Fall Leaf Stationary, 53–55
Pasta
  Halloween Ravioli with Red Pepper
    Sauce, 177
  Savory Noodle Kugel, 20
  Turkey with Spinach Tortellini and
    Fresh Oranges, 40
Pears
  Fennel and Pear Salad, 31
  Harvest "Thyme" Squash Soup, 23
  Roasted Pears with Sherry Apricot
    Sauce, 185
Peony, 131, 132
Perennials
  anemone, 116
  asters, 116–117
  boltonia, 117
  bugbane, 117
  geranium, 117
  globe thistle, 117–118

  goldenrod, 118
  helenium, 118
  helianthus, 118
  Joe Pye weed, 118–119
  lilyturf, 119
  planting for late-season blooming,
    117–119
  rudbeckia, 119
  sedum, 119
  sweet autumn clematis, 117
  toad lilies, 119
Pineapple
  Warm Ginger Pineapple Sauce on
    Vanilla Ice Cream, 168
Pizza
  Mediterranean Pizza, 164
Plant Now for Season-Long Bloom,
  130–135
Plastic mulch, 127
Pork Chops with Dried-Apple Stuffing, 36
Potatoes
  Baked Sweet Potato Spears, 184
  Roasted Poblano and Chile Mashes
    Potatoes, 16
  Yukon Gold Mashed Potatoes, 160
Potpourri, 121
Pots
  Fall Leaf Clay Pot, 74–75
Pumpkin
  Fajita Chicken in Pumpkin-Seed Sauce,
    34
  Pumpkin Swirl Cheesecake, 45
Pumpkin Container with Mum Plant,
  97–99
Pumpkin Swirl Cheesecake, 45
Puttanesca-Style Tomato Topping, 152

R

Raised beds, 126
Red and White Endive Slaw with Walnuts
  and Apples, 29
Red Onion Pickles Topping, 150
Red Twig Dogwood Bush, 76–77
Rice
  Curried Pilaf Salad, 28
  Thanksgiving Salad, 21
Roast Chicken, 38
Roasted Pears with Sherry Apricot Sauce,
  185
Roasted Poblano and Chile Mashes
  Potatoes, 16
Rocky Mountain region
  wildflowers for, 125
Root Vegetable and Barley Soup, 25
Rudbeckia, 119
Rustic Apple Tart, 161

S

Salads
 Caesar Salad, 26
 Curried Pilaf Salad, 28
 Fennel and Pear Salad, 31
 Hazelnut-Crusted Goat Cheese Rounds
  with Mixed Greens, 182
 Hot Pastrami Salad, 41
 Lox and Bagel Salad, 10
 Red and White Endive Slaw with
  Walnuts and Apples, 29
 Thanksgiving Salad, 21
Salsa Shrimp with Feta, 166
Sandwiches
 Turkey Club with Cranberry and BLT,
  33
Sauces
 Roasted Pears with Sherry Apricot
  Sauce, 185
 Sautéed Duck Breasts with Balsamic
  Sauce, 181
 Warm Ginger Pineapple Sauce on
  Vanilla Ice Cream, 168
Sautéed Duck Breasts with Balsamic
 Sauce, 181
Savory Noodle Kugel, 20
Scarecrow Wall Hanging, 68–70
Sedum, 119
Sewing projects
 Fall Chair Dressing, 109–111
 Fall Guest Hand Towel, 91–93
 Halloween Trick-or-Treat Bag, 65–67
Six Ways to Extend Your Veggie-Growing
 Season, 126–127
Smoked Salmon Pâté, 180
Snowdrop, 133
Soil
 fall soil prep tip, 129
Soups
 Harvest "Thyme" Squash Soup, 23
 Root Vegetable and Barley Soup, 25
 Squash Bisque, 156
Southeast region
 wildflowers for, 125
South region
 trees for fall color, 140
Southwest region
 wildflowers for, 125
Spider lily, 133–134
Spreads. See Dips and spreads
Squash
 Harvest "Thyme" Squash Soup, 23
 Squash Bisque, 156
Squash Bisque, 156
Stamping

Fall Leaf Stationary, 53–55
Storage and display
 Antique Potpourri Jar, 80–82
 Birdhouse Shoe Rack, 83–87
 Fall Leaf Clay Pot, 74–75
 Halloween Trick-or-Treat Bag, 65–67
 Mini-Kindling Box, 62–64
 Nature's Bounty Basket, 59–61
 Pumpkin Container with Mum Plant,
  97–99
Stuffing
 Pork Chops with Dried-Apple Stuffing,
  36
Sweet Autumn Clematis, 117

T

Table covering
 Fallen Leaves Table Topper, 103–105
Take It Easy This Fall, 162–168
 Couscous with Pine Nuts, 167
 Mediterranean Pizza, 164
 Salsa Shrimp with Feta, 166
 Warm Ginger Pineapple Sauce on
  Vanilla Ice Cream, 168
Tarts
 Rustic Apple Tart, 161
Thanksgiving Salad, 21
Toad lilies, 119
Tomatoes
 Herbed Tomato Gratin, 24
 Mexican Copanata, 14
 Puttanesca-Style Tomato Topping, 152
Toppings. See Dips and spreads
Trees for Autumn Color, 138–141
Tropics/Subtropics region
 trees for fall color, 141
Tulips, 131–133
Turkey
 Root Vegetable and Barley Soup, 25
 Thanksgiving Salad, 21
 Turkey Club with Cranberry and BLT,
  33
 Turkey with Spinach Tortellini and
  Fresh Oranges, 40
Turkey Club with Cranberry and BLT, 33
Turkey with Spinach Tortellini and Fresh
 Oranges, 40

V

Vegetable gardens
 six ways to extend your growing
  season, 126–127
A Very Scary Affair, 170–177
 Bat Chips and Salsa, 172

Bread Stick Bones, 174
 Creepy Baked Apples, 176
 Halloween Ravioli with Red Pepper
  Sauce, 177
 White Chocolate Pretzel Ghosts, 175
Vinaigrette. See Dressing/vinaigrette

W

Wall hangings
 Scarecrow Wall Hanging, 68–70
Warm Ginger Pineapple Sauce on Vanilla
 Ice Cream, 168
Weeds
 lawn fall tip, 128
 tips for managing weeds in wildflower
  garden, 123
West region
 wildflowers for, 125
White Chocolate Pretzel Ghosts, 175
Wildflower garden, 122–125
 choosing mix for, 124
 list of best wildflowers by region, 125
 time for planting, 122–124
 tips for managing weeds in, 123
 tips for new meadow, 124
Wire crafts
 Wire Luminaria, 71–73
 Witch Mobile, 100–102
Wire Luminaria, 71–73
Witch Mobile, 100–102
Wood crafts
 Birdhouse Shoe Rack, 83–87
Mini-Kindling Box, 62–64
Wood hyacinths, 137
Wreaths and garlands
 Dried Apple Garland, 94–96
 Fall Balsam Wreath, 56–58

Y

Yukon Gold Mashed Potatoes, 160

Z

Zucchini
Salsa Shrimp with Feta, 166

RECIPE & ENTERTAINING NOTES

CRAFT & DECORATING NOTES